THE CATHOLIC UNIVERSITY OF AMERICA
CANON LAW STUDIES
No. 209

PROOF OF THE RECEPTION OF THE SACRAMENTS

AN HISTORICAL SYNOPSIS AND COMMENTARY

BY

REV. EUGENE H. SULLIVAN, S.T.L., J.C.L.
Priest of the Archdiocese of Philadelphia

A DISSERTATION

Submitted to the Faculty of the School of Canon Law of the Catholic University of America in Partial Fulfillment of the Requirements for the Degree of Doctor of Canon Law

THE CATHOLIC UNIVERSITY OF AMERICA PRESS
WASHINGTON, D. C.
1944

Nihil Obstat:
CLEMENS V. BASTNAGEL, S.T.L., J.U.D.
Censor Deputatus
Washingtonii, D. C. die VI Maii, 1944

Imprimatur:
D. CARD. DOUGHERTY
✠ *Archiepiscopus Philadelphiensis*
Philadelphiae, die VIII Maii, 1944

MURRAY & HEISTER, WASHINGTON, D. C.
Printed in the United States of America

 9

To
My Mother
and
Father

TABLE OF CONTENTS

PART TWO

CANONICAL COMMENTARY

FOREWORD

THE present study endeavors to present an historical and canonical treatment of the question of proof of the reception of the sacraments. It aims to illustrate the methods that may be utilized to prove the fact that one has received one or the other of the sacraments.

The question of proof is purely legal and is a matter which is of itself extrinsic both to the valid administration and to the valid reception of the sacraments. For example, the valid reception of the sacrament of baptism does not depend upon one's ability to demonstrate that fact. If the baptism was validly received, the status of the recipient in God's sight remains the same whether or not there is extant any evidence that the baptism has been conferred. The recipient's status in the Church, however, may be greatly affected by his ability to prove the fact of his baptism. The Church, as a perfect society, is entitled to exact from her members, when this is deemed necessary, proof of the fact that they have received a certain sacrament. This dissertation is confined to the question of fact, that is, to the matter of establishing proof of the liturgical celebration and consequent reception of the individual sacraments. It does not embrace a study of the elements which are required for the valid administration and reception of each one of the sacraments.

The question which is treated here entails an investigation of the various agencies of proof which the law makes available for one who is called upon to establish, with convincing evidence, the fact that he has received this or that sacrament. If the legislator is to demand proof of this reception at a later date, then it logically follows that the law must determine what shall constitute adequate evidence of this fact and further must provide some stable agency of proof to which one may appeal. Canon Law fulfills the latter duty by its regulations governing the maintenance of official records of the administration of the sacraments.

In addition to a consideration of the different forms of proof, special instances wherein the law requests proof that a sacrament has been received will also be matter for discussion. These cases are pertinent, for sometimes the lawgiver not only states that proof must be furnished but also determines the type of proof which is required. In these circumstances the subject of the law is granted no freedom of choice. The form of proof which he must present will not be that which is most convenient for him to secure, but the particular one stipulated by official precept.

As is indicated in the Table of Contents, this work is divided into two general sections. The first section traces briefly the historical development of ecclesiastical law upon this question. The second section is devoted to a canonical commentary on the current law.

The writer wishes to express his gratitude to His Eminence, Dennis Cardinal Dougherty, Archbishop of Philadelphia, for the opportunity of advanced study in Canon Law; to the Faculty of the School of Canon Law; and to all others who contributed by their interest and aid towards the completion of this dissertation.

PART ONE

HISTORICAL SYNOPSIS

CHAPTER I

Introduction

The amount of historical material having direct reference to the subject of this dissertation is not so vast in the early centuries of the Church's history as to warrant that a special section be devoted to its consideration. This is not to say that there were no laws in regard to proof of the reception of the sacraments in the early period of ecclesiastical law. Some of the decrees which treat of this matter are of very ancient origin. These decrees have not been overlooked, but are considered as they make their appearance in the later development of law, namely in the collection of Gratian and in the law of the Papal Decretals.

There are definite stages discernible in the gradual development of law upon the question of proving the reception of the sacraments. Under the particular aspect of their proof those sacraments which in addition to their primary effect of conferring grace upon the recipient have also a social significance were the first to become the object of the law. Thus the fact that a person receives baptism affects not only the individual himself but also his association with others and with the society which is the Church. Baptism is of supreme necessity to all for salvation, the means whereby one is granted membership in Christ's Church and the foundation of the other sacraments.[1] Proof that one has received baptism may often be required to assure one of his rights as a Catholic. Ecclesiastical authority may exact it before permitting him to perform some act in the Church, e.g., to receive

[1] Canons 87; 737, §1.

other sacraments. Consequently from early times there were laws regulating what evidence was required to establish the fact of baptism.

The sacrament of holy orders confers a position of authority in the Church upon its recipient.[2] The welfare of a society and the maintenance of public order demand that they alone who are lawfully deputed to do so be allowed to exercise authority. Consequently it may be necessary for the priest or other minister to establish, for the benefit of those who do not know him, his reception of the order which he claims to possess. The interest of the faithful, moreover, in the valid ministrations of the priest and the becoming reverence for the sacraments require that due precautions be taken to prevent anyone from attempting to perform the functions of the sacred ministry without the requisite power of orders. The early Councils of the Church, therefore, enacted necessary legislation which directed what proof had to be presented by one who claimed to have been ordained.

The union of a man and woman in marriage gives rise to definite social effects in both the Church and the community. It guarantees the children of the marriage their rights as legitimate heirs of their parents. Catholic marriage joins the parties to each other for life, at the same time making it impossible for them, while they are both alive, to form a like union with another. Among other questions which law must clarify in regard to marriage is that which touches upon the proof of its existence. The preservation of a good reputation as well as the benefits to be acquired for themselves or for their children may be contingent upon the ability of a man and woman to substantiate with convincing proof their reception of the sacrament of matrimony. For these reasons norms concerning proof of the reception of this sacrament were also well outlined before the Council of Trent (1545–1563).

Beginning with the Council of Trent, historical data upon this subject became more abundant. Special laws were enacted bringing within their scope more of the individual sacraments. Prior to the Council particular regulations were made concerning only

---

[2] Canon 948.

three of the sacraments, namely, baptism, matrimony and holy orders, as touching upon the proof of their reception. The post-Tridentine period saw the law expanded to embrace other sacraments as well, in the matter of such regulations.

For another reason also the Council of Trent marks a turning point in the history of this topic. Prior to the Council the most forceful probative value was vested in testimonial proof. Since little credence was given to any public records that may have existed, the proof by means of witnesses was utilized almost exclusively. From the time of the Council of Trent, however, until the present Code of Canon Law the tendency of the law has been to place greater emphasis upon documentary evidence. This trend is traceable to the legislation respecting the keeping of parochial records, which was initiated at the Council of Trent. After the custody of certain authentic records in all parishes became an object of universal ecclesiastical law, testimonial evidence was forced to assume a subsidiary character. These parochial registers were designed to be an authentic record of one's having received a certain sacrament. The history of the proof of the reception of the sacraments, therefore, is necessarily closely allied during this period with the development of the system of parish registers.

The present Code of Canon Law in its legislation governing proof of the reception of the sacraments follows closely the principles which were a part of canonical jurisprudence before the Code. The new law is not a radical departure from the old, but for the most part an authoritative confirmation of the usage and practice that were in existence before its promulgation. Consequently a better understanding of the current legislation is obtained if it is considered in the light of its earlier development and in view of the motives which prompted its enactment.

CHAPTER II

The Law of the *Corpus Iuris Canonici*

Article 1. Baptism

The question of what evidence was required to prove one's reception of the sacrament of baptism was treated most explicitly in the Decree of Gratian. The norms were given relative to the solution of the problem of when it was licit to baptize those whose baptism could not be established with any degree of certainty. Gratian († 1140) considered a practical case.

A number of children were returned to their own country after having lived in captivity among barbarians. No one was available who could testify to their baptism and the children themselves could supply no information. What was to be done?

Pope Gregory II (715–731) in the year 726 determined that in such a case, in accord with what had been handed down by tradition, these children should be baptized, since there was no one who could testify to their baptism.[1] This law asserted how proof for the baptism could be established. The fact of the reception of baptism could be juridically established by witnesses who testified to that effect.

Gratian quoted a similar prescription taken from the V Council of Carthage (circa 401 during the reign of Pope Anastasius I 398–401) which stated that children should be baptized whenever it was impossible to ascertain whether they had been baptized

[1] C. 110, D. IV, *de cons.—Corpus Iuris Canonici* (ed. Lipsiensis 2. post Aemilii Ludovici Richteri curas instruxit Aemilius Friedberg, 2 vols., Lipsiae: Ex Officina Bernhardi Tauchnitz, 1879–1881. Editio anastatice repetita, Lipsiae: Tauchnitz, 1928). (This edition will be used exclusively, except for citations from the *Glossae* which will be taken from the Roman edition.) *Jaffé, Regesta Pontificum Romanorum ab condita Ecclesia ad annum post Christum natum MCXCVIII* (ed. 2, Kaltenbrunner, Ewald, Loewenfeld), 2 vols. in 1, Lipsiae, 1885–1888), n. 2174 (hereafter cited as Jaffé); Mansi, *Sacrorum Conciliorum Nova et Amplisima Collectio* (53 vols. in 60, Parisiis, 1901–1927), XII, 246 (this work will be henceforth cited as Mansi).

in view of the fact that witnesses were lacking and the children themselves could not remember.[2] This conciliar legislation requires "*certissimi testes,*" presumably at least two or more witnesses. In both of the canons cited by Gratian the sole method of proof suggested is the testimony of witnesses, that is, persons who can testify unqualifiedly that the person in question has been baptized.

A succeeding canon in the *Decree* of Gratian gives information as to who would be the most likely individuals capable of supplying the desired testimony. These witnesses are to be sought among relatives, servants, neighbors and the priests.[3] The most certain method of establishing the fact that baptism had been conferred was, therefore, recourse to a plurality of witnesses to be looked for among the immediate family or the priests. The testimony which such witnesses could offer was legitimate proof of one's baptism.

Although the testimony of a number of witnesses was considered to be of the greatest value, it was not the only proof admitted. The testimony rendered by one witness alone was also accepted as adequate proof of the reception of this sacrament. This is the rule which Pope Leo I (440–461) enunciated in a letter to the Bishop of Ravenna.[4]

The admission of the testimony of one witness as a sufficient proof of one's baptism seems to be an exception to the general norm that required always at least more than one witness to establish any given fact. The principle of Roman law was "*unus testis, nullus testis.*"[5] This same principle found its way into the law of the Church. Examples of its application are to be

---

[2] C. 111, D. IV; *de cons.;* V Council of Carthage, can. 6—Mansi, III, 967.

[3] C. 113, D. IV, *de cons.* (this is taken from a letter of Pope Leo I [440–461] to Bishop Rusticus of Narbonne in the year 458–459); Jaffé, n. 544; Mansi, VI, 397.

[4] "Cum itaque baptismi sui nihil recordetur, qui regenerationis est cupidus nec alter de eo attestari possit . . . atque ideo quociens persona talis inciderit, solicita primum examinatione discutite et longo tempore (nisi supremus finis immineat) indagate, utrum nemo penitus sit qui testimonio suo iuvare possit ignorantiam nescientis . . ."—c. 112, D. IV, *de cons.;* Jaffé, n. 543; Mansi, VI, 387. (This was written in the year 458.)

[5] C (4,20) 9.

found in Gratian as well as in the Decretals of Gregory IX.[6] Such a derogation from the general norm could not have been permitted indiscriminately. It would seem that when credence was given to the testimony of one witness, special qualifications must have been exacted of him. This supposition is justified by an examination of the *Glossa Ordinaria* to the canons under consideration.[7]

The Glossator states explicitly that the testimony of one witness may establish the fact of baptism. He notes that in this respect baptism differs from holy orders. To prove one's ordination more is required.[8] He goes on to consider a hypothetical case. Could an individual testify to his baptism if he would thereby receive a certain legacy, precisely on the condition that he had been baptized? The testimony of the one witness could not be accepted in such a case, he concludes, because such testimony might be prejudicial to a rightful heir.[9] Another gloss demands that in the event that there is only one witness, this witness must be a Christian, and not a pagan or a Jew.[10] If the testimony of one witness therefore was to be accepted as full proof of the reception of baptism, this witness had to be above all suspicion and his testimony had to be of such a nature as not to prejudice the rights of another or to benefit an interested party.

This one witness, it would seem, could even have been the individual himself whose baptism was under question.[11] The Glossator does not exclude the possibility of one's testifying concerning things that occurred in childhood.[12] If the baptism had been conferred in adult years there would have been no reason to deny one's testimony to that effect, provided that the above mentioned conditions required in a single witness had been fulfilled.

From the foregoing it can be readily seen that under the old

---

[6] C. 11, C. XXXV, q. 6; c. 22, X, *de testibus et attestationibus*, II, 20.

[7] *Glossa Ord.* ad cc. 111, 112, D. IV, *de cons.*

[8] *Glossa Ord.* ad c. 111, D. IV, *de cons.*, s. v. *testentur.*

[9] *Glossa Ord.* ad c. 111, D. IV, *de cons.*, s. v. *testentur.*

[10] *Glossa Ord.* ad c. 112, D. IV, *de cons.*, s. v. *qui testimonio.*

[11] Cc. 111, 112, D. IV, *de cons.*

[12] *Glossa Ord.* ad c. 112, D. IV, *de cons.*, s. v. *Qui testimonio.*

Church law the reception of baptism was a fact that had to be proved. It was not gratuitously presumed. This was in accord with the general jurisprudence of the times. Facts had to be proved.[13] The reception of the sacrament of baptism could be substantiated by the testimony of witnesses, preferably a plurality of them, but that failing, by at least one who was recognized to be above all suspicion—even the person himself whose baptism was the subject of discussion.

The next question that immediately comes to mind is presumption regarding the fact of baptism. Was the fact of baptism ever presumed? Did the law provide for the case where the requisite witnesses could not be found? Was it ever allowable to presume that baptism had been conferred, when witnesses could not be produced to testify in favor of the reception of this sacrament?

Gratian and the Decretals give evidence that in certain specific cases it could be rightfully presumed that baptism was administered. One example is to be found in the *Decree* of Gratian.[14] When the fact of baptism was doubtful and could not be proved in the usual manner, the person was to be questioned as to whether he could ever recall having gone to church with his parents and having received the Blessed Sacrament. A presumption was thus established that if he had been granted permission to receive Holy Communion he must have been baptized.[15]

The Decretals of Gregory IX point out another presumption in favor of baptism received, wider in scope than the previous one. This presumption was placed in favor of a child of good Catholic parentage. The Catholicity of the parents in such circumstances took the place of the required proof of the child's baptism, which was lacking. A case was proposed to Pope Innocent III (1198–

[13] C. 75, C. XI, q. 3 (this is taken from St. Augustine's *Liber de penetencia,* a work of doubtful authenticity).

[14] C. 113, D. IV, *de cons.* (this is taken from a letter of Pope Leo I [440–461] to Bishop Rusticus of Narbonne in the year 458–459); Jaffé, n. 544.

[15] *Glossa Ord.* ad c. 113, D. IV, *de cons.,* s. v. *acceperint.* The Glossator specifically calls this a presumption.

1216) by a young man who, after he had received sacred orders, learned that he had not been baptized.[16]

In a reply addressed to the Bishop of Ferrara the Pope directed that in accordance with the principle proposed by the Council of Compiègne (758)[17] the cleric should be baptized and reordained. The Pope concluded his response by saying that the baptism of one born and reared among Catholics is emphatically presumed. It is so strongly presumed that it is to be considered as certain until such time that the contrary would perhaps be proved by certain argumentation. What was the probative value of such a presumption? This presumption was a *praesumptio iuris* in Pope Innocent's decretal law. It was not a *praesumptio iuris et de iure,* for the law itself admitted of a contrary factual proof if the facts upon which such proof was based could be substantiated.[18] The *Glossa Ordinaria* written by Bernard of Parma († 1266) cites other usages in the law where similar strong presumptions gave way to certain contrary proof.[19]

It seems unusual that the law of the *Corpus Iuris Canonici* was silent on the question of proof from written records. The law itself, however, made no mention at all of any proof of the reception of baptism which might be drawn from written records either parochial or diocesan. Passing reference is made to the existence of some such records by Panormitanus (1386–1453), one of the Decretalists of the fifteenth century.[20] He admits of a proof of baptism based on what he calls the *libri ecclesiae.* The value which he concedes to these records, however, seems to be

---

[16] C. 3, X, *de presbytero non baptizato,* III, 43; Comp. III, c. 1, *h.t.* (5, 22); Potthast, *Regesta Pontificum Romanorum* (2 vols., Berolini: R. De Becker, 1874–1875), n. 2749 (hereafter cited as Potthast).

[17] Cf. c. 60, C. I, q. 1; Mansi, XII, 657.

[18] Cf. Wernz-Vidal, *Ius Canonicum* (7 vols. in 8, Romae: apud Aedes Universitatis Gregorianae, 1927–1938. Vol. I, 1938; Vol. II, 2. ed., 1928; Vol. III, 1933; Vol. IV, Pars I, 1934; Vol. IV, Pars II, 1935; Vol. V, 2. ed., 1928; Vol. VI, 1927; Vol. VII, 1937), VI, n. 518.

[19] *Glossa Ord.* ad c. 3, X, *de presbytero non baptizato,* III, 43, s. v. *contrarium probabitur.*

[20] Panormitanus (Nicholaus de Tudeschis), *Commentaria in Libros Decretalium* (Venetiis, apud Juntas, 1588), Lib. II, tit. *de probationibus, c.* 13, n. 1.

very insignificant. He calls these books unauthentic and the proof taken from them he designates as *non plena.* He concedes their power to prove the fact of baptism because in the particular proposed case there would be no fear of causing prejudice to another person's rights.[21] From the silence of the law itself on this point one may judge that this type of proof was rarely resorted to and would have been cautiously received, if at all, in a contentious trial. The keeping of parochial records did not become a subject of universal legislation until the Council of Trent.[22]

ARTICLE 2. HOLY ORDERS

The jurisprudence of the *Corpus Iuris Canonici* takes cognizance of the problem of the proof of the reception of sacred orders. The regulations regarding the proof that was required to substantiate the fact of one's ordination are prescribed in connection with the question of how ecclesiastical superiors are to treat traveling clerics who come into their district.

Gratian collected three canons which describe the procedure to be followed in receiving unknown members of the clergy. One is a pseudo-Isidorian text attributed to Pope Sylvester I (314–337).[23] The other two are a letter of Pope Anastasius I (398–401) to all Bishops[24] and a letter of Pope Gregory I (590–604) to the Bishop of Squillace.[25] These canons commanded the bishops not to receive into their dioceses clerics who came from remote regions unless the clerics could show testimonial letters inscribed with the seals of five bishops attesting the fact of their ordination.

When seeking permanent admission into a diocese other than his own a cleric was required to produce *litterae commendatitiae.* Gratian incorporated several canons treating of these letters into

---

[21] *Commentaria,* Lib. II, tit. *de probationibus,* c. 13, n. 1.

[22] Wernz, *Ius Decretalium* (6 vols., Romae: Ex Typographia Polyglotta, 1906–1913), IV, p. 315, n. 197.

[23] C. 1, D. XCVIII; Hinschius, *Decretales Pseudo-Isidorianae et Capitula Angilramni* (Ex Officina Bernhardi Tauchnitz, Lipsiae, 1863), p. 451.

[24] C. 2, D. XCVIII; Jaffé, n. 277; Mansi, III, 940 (the exact date of this letter is unknown).

[25] C. 3, D. XCVIII; Jaffé, n. 1191 (this was written in 592).

his *Decretum*. They are also called *litterae dimissoriales* or *litterae formatae*.[26] Gratian used these terms indiscriminately. They were dimissorial letters, therefore, but the term did not have the same significance in Gratian or the Decretals as it has in the present law. These letters were letters of permanent incardination, as can be seen from the model which Gratian listed.[27] The Council of Chalcedon (451) stated that no cleric should be allowed to function in a diocese other than his own without these letters of dismissal from his own bishop.[28] The I Council of Carthage (348) gave a similar prescription.[29]

By means of both the *litterae testimoniales* and the *litterae dimissoriales* the cleric was enabled to prove his status to the satisfaction of superiors whom he would encounter upon entering foreign dioceses. The meaning and use of these letters became clearer in decretal law.

In the Decretals of Pope Gregory IX (1227–1241) under the title, *De Clericis Peregrinis,* the matter of substantiating the fact of one's ordination is considered.[30] These regulations are again treated in connection with the question of how ecclesiastical superiors are to treat traveling clerics who come into their district. The general norm which these laws inculcate is to the effect that traveling members of the clergy are not to be promoted to higher orders or allowed the exercise of the orders they claim to have already received until they adequately prove that they are legitimately ordained.

Hostiensis († 1271) assigns four reasons for this legislation:

(1) Were a bishop to ordain one who is not his subject without permission he would intrude upon another's jurisdiction.

(2) *Peregrini* are frequently excommunicated or otherwise irregular.

(3) Such persons often lay claim to orders which they do not possess, or they desire to be incorporated into higher orders than they merit.

---

[26] C. 1, D. LXXIII.

[27] C. 1, D. LXXIII.

[28] C. 7, D. LXXI; Mansi, VII, 418.

[29] C. 6, D. LXXI; Mansi, III, 155.

[30] Cc. 1, 2, 3, X, *de clericis peregrinis,* I, 22.

(4) If traveling clerics are unable to show a grant of permission to depart from their own dioceses, they are to be presumed disobedient, since it is not lawful for any cleric to be outside of his own diocese without the consent of his bishop.[31]

The first of the letters in the title *De Clericis Peregrinis* is a response of Pope Alexander III (1159–1181) to the Bishop of Le Mans.[32] The problem for which the bishop asked a solution concerned clerics who travel into regions where they are unknown. They say that they are ordained, but produce no documents from the bishop who ordained them. What is to be the procedure in such circumstances? The Pope in his reply urged a careful observance of what had already been prescribed in this regard. He stated it to be a command that, when clerics come from remote regions into sections where they are not known, they should provide themselves with testimonial letters inscribed with the seals of five bishops attesting the fact of their ordination. Such clerics, moreover, are to be kept under surveillance for some time in order that those with whom they associate may have an opportunity to estimate their worth. Furthermore, inquiry is to be instituted in order to make certain that all intervening minor orders have been canonically received. Pope Alexander III in this letter merely repeated the already extant law found in Gratian's collection and advised its observance.[33]

The Glossator in his commentary gives an elucidation of this law of Alexander III which Gregory IX inserted in the Decretals. The seals of five bishops are required, he says, with the end in view that all possibility of fraud may be obviated. If it were entirely clear that no deception was present the seal of one bishop alone would suffice.[34] Hostiensis concurs in this, for he exacts the seals of five bishops only in the event that the seal of the cleric's own bishop is unknown to the bishop into whose diocese the cleric seeks admission. If the cleric had a testimonial letter

---

[31] Hostiensis (Henricus de Segusia), *Summa Aurea* (Venetiis, 1570), Lib. I, tit. *de clericis peregrinis*, n. 2.

[32] C. 1, X, *de clericis peregrinis*, I, 22; Comp. I, c. 1, *h.t.* (1, 14); Jaffé, n. 13842 (the exact date of this letter is unknown).

[33] Cf. *Glossa Ord.* ad c. 1, X, *de clericis peregrinis*, I, 22, s. v. *statutum*.

[34] *Glossa Ord.* ad c. 1, X, *de clericis peregrinis*, I, 22, s. v. *quinque*.

signed with the seal of his own bishop, and this seal was familiar to the receiving bishop, the candidate could be accepted. In such circumstances the bishop could easily verify the authenticity of the letter.[35] Practically, then, the very old law requiring five seals had been abandoned at the time of the Decretals. The Glossator also observed that the period of probation mentioned in the law was only to be applied to those who wished to exercise their ministry publicly. If they merely desired to celebrate Mass privately they were allowed to do so.[36] The case which this law contemplated appeared then to be that in which the cleric was a *peregrinus* in the strict acceptance of the word. He was absent from his diocese but did not intend to remain absent permanently.

One's claim to sacred orders, therefore, was not readily accepted unless he was able to substantiate his contention with evidence of a particular nature. A similar norm was prescribed by Pope Innocent III (1198–1216) in reply to a question proposed by the Latin Patriarch of Constantinople. This Patriarchate had been created during the Crusades and there was an urgent demand for Latin clerics in the new dioceses of the Orient. The Patriarch, therefore, inquired about clerics who came into his territory, offering to take an oath that they had received this or that order, but having no letter to that effect. Was their oath to be accepted and could they then be promoted to higher orders? The Pope replied that their oath should not be accepted as a proof that they had received orders, nor was it permissible to promote them to higher orders until they could prove their canonical ordination by reliable evidence (*idonea argumenta*).[37] This law added something to the prior one in that it definitely excluded the possibility of proving the fact of ordination by the taking of an oath. An oath did not furnish recognized proof in this case.

By the expression *idonea argumenta* the Glossator understands indications which would lead one to give credence to the cleric's assertion, such as the *sigilla episcoporum* mentioned in the pre-

---

[35] *Summa Aurea,* Lib. I, tit. *de clericis peregrinis,* n. 3.

[36] *Glossa Ord.* ad c. 1, X, *de clericis peregrinis,* I, 22, 3, s. v. *in suspensione.*

[37] C. 2, X, *de clericis peregrinis,* I, 22; Comp. III, c. 1, *h.t.* (1, 16); Potthast, n. 2860 (this was written in the year 1206).

ceding canon. If the document was lost, then the owner not only had to prove this loss, but he had to establish the content of the document and also that it was not for some reason purposely destroyed.[38]

An examination of the gloss further reveals that the letters which the cleric should have when asking admission to another diocese are those which were called *litterae commendaticiae* and which were described by Gratian.[39] Hostiensis defined these letters as constituting the method by which a bishop released someone from his power and jurisdiction and gave him permission to transfer to whatever other place he wished.[40] They had the force of permanently dissociating a cleric from service in a given diocese and of leaving him free to join another. Without such authorization from his bishop, no other bishop could accept the cleric for service in his church.[41] This procedure was the usual way in which the law provided for the permanent departure of a cleric from his diocese and his consequent enrollment in another bishop's jurisdiction. The letters of dismissal were utilized for a twofold purpose:

(1) They served to excardinate the cleric, and (2) They gave a full report on his status by certifying to any orders he had received and by indicating any irregularity to which perhaps he was subject.

So far the only evidence recognized as being sufficient proof of one's ordination was of a documentary type—a testimony of orders received, or dimissorial letters for a permanent attachment to a foreign diocese. Was this the only evidence acceptable, or was oral testimony also of some value as proof? The final canon in the title *de clericis peregrinis* admitted proof also by means of witnesses. This is a letter of Pope Innocent III to the Patriarch of Jerusalem in the year 1207.[42] The Glossator takes this in a broad interpretation as meaning that any legitimate proof, so

[38] *Glossa Ord.* ad c. 2, X, *de clericis peregrinis,* I, 22, s. v. *per argumenta.*

[39] *Glossa Ord.* ad c. 2, X, *de clericis peregrinis,* I, 22, s. v. *litteris.*

[40] *Summa Aurea,* Lib. I, tit. *de clericis peregrinis,* n. 4.

[41] Cf. cc. 6, 7, D. LXXI.

[42] C. 3, X, *de clericis peregrinis,* I, 22; Comp. III, c. 2, *h.t.* (1, 16); Potthast, n. 2994.

long as it is unmistakably clear, will suffice.[43] This canon also repeats that some proof is required only when the priest wishes to celebrate Mass publicly. If he wishes to celebrate privately, he may be allowed to do so without producing the accustomed proof. The Glossator explains the reason for this distinction. If the cleric is in reality not a duly ordained priest, then in celebrating privately he will do harm to no one other than himself. If, however, he is not ordained and offers Mass publicly, then the people also would be deceived.[44]

The norms which the *Corpus Iuris Canonici* indicates for establishing proof of the reception of holy orders may be summarized in the following manner:

(1) The reception of any order was a fact which had to be proved to the satisfaction of ecclesiastical superiors. Members of the clergy who traveled to Christian communities where they were not known were not received unless they were capable of supporting the claims they made.

(2) The standard proof under the law was documentary evidence. If a cleric was to be permanently connected with the service of a bishop other than his own, he had to produce letters of dismissal from his own bishop. This document furnished proof for the existence of the orders he had already received. If he was not permanently residing in a foreign diocese, then a testimony of ordination inscribed with the seal of five bishops, or at least of one bishop, provided that there was no doubt as to its authenticity, entitled him to exercise publicly the functions of his respective order.

(3) If such documents were unobtainable, the proof of ordination could be established by witnesses.

(4) An oath alone was not regarded as a valid proof of the reception of orders.

This matter was not considered in any later legislation of the *Corpus Iuris Canonici.*

---

[43] ". . . *per testes vel per alia legitima argumenta* . . ."—*Glossa Ord.* ad c. 3, X, *de clericis peregrinis,* I, 22, s. v. *per testes.*

[44] *Glossa Ord.* ad c. 3, X, *de clericis peregrinis,* I, 22, s. v. *secreto,*

ARTICLE 3. MATRIMONY

The sacrament of matrimony occupies a prominent place in the law of the *Corpus Iuris Canonici*. In this as in other periods of ecclesiastical law marriage was the object of abundant legislation. The canonists during this time were especially preoccupied with the question of proof for the contraction of marriage. Commentators generally trace this to the difficulty of proving the existence of the clandestine marriage.[45] Canonists of the Decretal period had to concern themselves with the clandestine marriage no less than with the public marriage. For this reason the question of proof for the contraction of marriage became a complicated matter.

A. The Form of Marriage

In the law of the *Corpus Iuris Canonici* the manner in which the marriage was celebrated had a definite bearing on how the existence of the marriage could be proved. At that time the mode of celebration or the exchange of consent was not always performed under like circumstances. Consequently it will be enlightening to consider briefly how marriage was accustomed to be celebrated.

The Germanic peoples, after their conversion to Catholicism, generally celebrated marriage at the door of the church, literally *in facie ecclesiae,* after which the married couple entered the church to attend Mass and receive Holy Communion. Among the various solemnities of the marriage ceremony was the nuptial blessing by the priest.[46] The law itself makes various references to these established customs.[47] The marriage question of King

---

[45] De Smet, *De Sponsalibus et Matrimonio* (4. ed., Brugis: Car. Beyaert, 1927), n. 149; Wernz, *Ius Decretalium,* IV, p. 298, n. 187; Esmein, *Le Mariage En Droit Canonique* (2. ed., 2 vols., Paris: Recueil Sirey. Vol. I, ed. R. Genestal, 1929; Vol. II, ed. R. Genestal–J. Dauvillier, 1935), II, 214; Wernz-Vidal, *Ius Canonicum,* V, n. 580.

[46] Wernz, *Ius Decretalium,* IV, pp. 216–217, *n.* 156; Esmein, *Le Marriage En Droit Canonique,* I, 198–199.

[47] C. 28, X, *de sponsalibus et matrimonio,* IV, 1 (Honorius III refers to the blessing at the door of the church). C. 17, C. XXVIII, q. 1, *in dictis* (Gratian speaks of the necessity of the priestly blessing).

Lothar II of Lorraine (855–869) illustrates the prevailing custom of the early middle ages. Pope Nicholas I (858–867) had instructed the legates whom he sent to investigate the case to inquire whether the marriage had been entered into before witnesses, according to the law and with the blessing of the priest.[48] This was the public celebration of marriage.

Opposed to this was the clandestine marriage. The word "clandestine," as applied to marriage, had various significations in the course of the centuries. In its original meaning it pointed to a marriage contracted without witnesses and for which there was no testimony other than the word of the parties themselves.[49] After the IV General Council of the Lateran (1215) a marriage was called clandestine when the banns, the publication of which was prescribed by that Council, were omitted.[50] This Council reiterated a long standing ecclesiastical prohibition against clandestine marriages, ordered the banns of all marriages to be published, and forbade priests to assist at marriages that were not contracted publicly. Gregory IX included this canon of the IV Lateran Council in his decretal collection.[51]

Despite the ecclesiastical prescription of public marriage and the frequent prohibition against clandestine marriage, it was generally admitted that there was no law invalidating the clandestine celebration of marriage until the decree "*Tametsi*" of the Council of Trent.[52] Consequently throughout the period of Gratian and the Decretals, the clandestine marriage, though forbidden, was not denied possible validity. For this reason canonists had to take cognizance of the proof of the contraction of a clandestine marriage. Perhaps Gratian best summarized the attitude of the law in respect to clandestine marriages. He did not deny that

---

[48] C. 4, C. XXXI, q. 2; Jaffé, n. 2726 (this was written in 863).

[49] De Smet, *De Sponsalibus et Matrimonio*, n. 159. (The word "clandestine" will be used in this sense.)

[50] IV Lateran Council, c. 51—Mansi, XXII, 1038; Comp. IV, c. un. *de clandestina desponsatione* (4, 2).

[51] C. 3, X, *de clandestina desponsatione*, IV, 3.

[52] Hostiensis, *Summa Aurea*, Lib. IV, tit. *de clandestina desponsatione*, n. 5; Wernz, *Ius Decretalium*, IV, p. 229, n. 158; De Smet, *De Sponsalibus et Matrimonio*, n. 104; Esmein, *Le Mariage En Droit Canonique*, I, 199.

they were valid if their contraction was proved by the confession of the parties. He showed, however, why ecclesiastical authority had to condemn them. If one of the contracting parties to a clandestine marriage forsook that union to enter a public marriage, then the other party was without means of proving that they had been previously validly married. The judge, who was forced to be guided by the evidence at hand, of necessity had to pronounce his sentence in favor of the validity of the public marriage.[53] It was because of the many difficulties attendant upon proving the existence of these clandestine unions that the lawmakers of the Church saw fit to forbid them.

B. Proof of the Contraction of Public Marriage

When marriage was celebrated publicly in accordance with law, how could the fact of its celebration be proved? The type of proof which seems to have enjoyed the foremost rank was the testimony of witnesses who had been in attendance at the marriage ceremony. There are two decretal letters which inculcate this doctrine. The first is a letter of Pope Honorius III (1216–1227), in which the Pope decided that the testimony of witnesses to a marriage should prevail over the woman's denial of having given her consent in marriage.[54] The text requires only *testes legitimi et idonei;* hence two witnesses seem to have constituted a sufficient number. Panormitanus († 1453), adhering to this opinion, based his contention on the fifteenth rule of law of Boniface VIII, *Pluralis locutio duorum numero est contenta.*[55]

Innocent III (1198–1216) rendered a similar decision when he recognized the celebration of a marriage inasmuch as there was proof of its celebration in the fact of witnesses who had been present, even though local gossip pointed to the union as merely concubinage.[56] The proof through the aid of witnesses was, therefore, the most valuable manner of substantiating the recep-

---

[53] *Dicta post* cc. 9, 11, C. XXX, q. 5.

[54] C. 28, X, *de sponsalibus et matrimonio,* IV, 1: Comp. V, c. 2, *h.t.* (4, 1); Potthast, n. 6106. (This was written in 1219.)

[55] *Commentaria,* Lib. IV, tit. *de sponsalibus et matrimonio,* C. 28, n. 3.

[56] C. 12, X, *qui filii sint legitimi,* IV, 17; Comp. III, c. 1, *h.t.* (4, 12); Potthast, n. 338. (This was written in 1198.)

tion of the sacrament of matrimony. The sources do not give very much information regarding what was required of these witnesses. They certainly had to comply with the general norms regulating the matter of proof by witnesses. The Glossator notes that they were placed under oath when testifying.[57]

It seems that one of the Decretals may be correctly interpreted to mean that the parents of the interested parties were permitted to testify for or against the existence of the marriage contract. This is a letter of Celestine I (422–432) to the Bishop of Florence, in which letter it was stated that relatives and parents were authorized to testify concerning a possible impediment of consanguinity in marriage cases.[58] The Glossator, so it appears, was of the persuasion that the parents could be permitted to testify only concerning the consanguinity.[59] Hostiensis also was of this opinion.[60] Panormitanus, on the contrary, claimed that parents were permitted to testify even when there was question of whether a marriage had been contracted. He advanced the cogent reason that the parents were the ones most likely to have been present at the marriage, and consequently they were to be allowed to testify to it unless the judge for some reason suspected their testimony.[61]

Another mode of proof for the celebration of a marriage that immediately suggests itself is the proof which is drawn from written records in the various local parishes where the marriages were celebrated. As has been stated, the law of the *Corpus Iuris Canonici* made no provisions for the keeping of parochial registers. An examination of the law itself nowhere reveals any mention of the records of marriage. This leads one to suppose that such

---

[57] *Glossa Ord.*, ad c. 28, X, *de sponsalibus et matrimonio,* IV, 1, s. v. *assertio.*

[58] C. 3, X, *qui matrimonium accusare possunt vel contra illud testari,* IV, 18; Jaffé, n. 384. (The exact date when this was written is not known. The rubric attributes it to Clement III [1187–1191].)

[59] *Glossa Ord.* ad c. 3, X, *qui matrimonium accusare possunt vel contra illud testari,* IV, 18, s. v. *sciunt.*

[60] *Commentaria in Libros Decretalium* (Venetiis, 1581), Lib. IV, tit. *qui matrimonium accusare possunt,* c. II, n. 1.

[61] *Commentaria,* Lib. IV, tit. *qui matrimonium accusare possunt,* c. III, n. 3.

records were not universally kept, and as a result not generally invoked, to prove the existence of a marital union. Among the commentators passing mention is made of such records. Hostiensis, in speaking of the nuptial blessing, insisted that nothing be exacted for it or for the document.[62]

Since no further description is given, it is difficult to ascertain what he intended by the word *charta*. Panormitanus discussed more in detail the proof taken from the *libri ecclesiarum*. If no prejudice to anyone was involved and a *probatio non plena* sufficed, then these books could be accepted as furnishing the requisite proof. If, however, it was a case which perhaps prejudiced the right of another, then these books were of no value unless they were very ancient, highly reputed and preserved in a place where authentic documents were kept.[63] Consequently, in any dispute over the proof for the celebration of a marriage these records could in all likelihood be easily ruled out by a judge. From the principles which Panormitanus proposed as well as from the law's silence in this regard one may justly conclude that these records were rarely used as proof and that full probative value was generally denied to them.

C. *Clandestine Marriage*

When marriage was contracted in a strictly clandestine fashion without any witnesses at all, it appears that the proof of its contraction depended to a great extent upon the confession of the parties themselves.

(a) The Confession of the Parties as a Means of Proof

If both parties published the celebration of a clandestine marriage, this marriage was ratified and approved by the Church as if it had been publicly contracted in the beginning. This was the doctrine of Alexander III (1159–1181), as expressed in a decretal

---

62 ". . . *Pro hac autem benedictione nihil exigi debet obtentu etiam alicujus consuetudinis nec pro charta. . . .*"—*Summa Aurea,* Lib. IV, tit. *de secundis nuptiis,* n. 3.

63 *Commentaria,* Lib. II, *de probationibus,* c. 13, n. 1.

letter to the Bishop of Beauvais.[64] The application of this general norm, however, did not always imply a legitimate proof. The dual confession of the celebration of a clandestine marriage could not prevail against the fact of a public marriage lawfully proved. The judge had to let the evidence which proved the fact of the public marriage guide him in making his decision.[65] Panormitanus stated the same principle, namely, that the confession of the celebration of a clandestine marriage did not prejudice the established fact of a public marriage.[66]

The previously cited decretal of Alexander III also provided another norm to be used in certifying the fact of a clandestine union. The denial on the part of both parties of such a marriage established proof of its non-existence. If both parties denied that they had contracted a clandestine marriage, then the law did not compel them to live as husband and wife. The same was true if only one party denied the existence of the marriage.[67] Perhaps the greatest juridical weakness attendant upon the legal recognition accorded to clandestine marriage was that the marriage could be so easily repudiated by one or the other of the parties. Only if the party who did not wish to abandon the marriage could prove that the marriage had been contracted did the mere denial of the other party lack sufficient force to dissolve the marriage.

In the event that one party asserted that marriage had been clandestinely contracted and the other party denied this testimony, it remained with the one who claimed that the marriage had taken place to prove this assertion. Upon failure to produce such proof each party was free to marry again.[68] This principle seems to be denied by another canon which St. Raymond of Penyafort (ca. 1175–1275) in his edition of the Decretals of Gregory IX allocated to a Council of Arles. It stated that if the man or woman

---

[64] C. 2, X, *de clandestina desponsatione,* IV, 3; Comp. I, c. 3, *h.t.* (4, 3); Jaffé, n. 1377. (The exact date of this letter is uncertain.)

[65] *Dicta post* cc. 9, 11, C. XXX, q. 5.

[66] *Commentaria,* Lib. IV, tit. *de clandestina desponsatione,* c. II, n. 6.

[67] C. 2, X, *de clandestina desponsatione,* IV, 3.

[68] Panormitanus, *Commentaria,* Lib. IV, tit. *de clandestina desponsatione,* c. II, n. 1; c. 28, X, *de sponsalibus et matrimonio,* IV, 1.

denied the clandestine marriage the burden of proof devolved upon the man.[69]

Presumably this canon placed upon the man the burden of either proving the existence of the marriage if the woman denied it, or of proving the non-existence of the marriage if the woman asserted the existence of the marriage and he denied it. The commentators endeavored to reconcile this canon with the general rule of law, *actori incumbit probatio,* that is, that the burden of proving the existence of the marriage rested upon the one who claimed that it had been contracted—either man or woman. Hostiensis said that the word *vir* is used here not in opposition to the word *mulier,* but to signify the one who took the virile rôle of proving the existence of the marriage.[70]

Panormitanus bears witness that the common teaching of the doctors was that the one who asserted the marriage had to prove its existence, whether it was the man or the woman. But he admits that this commonly accepted doctrine cannot be verified in this canon except by an improper use of the words of the text.[71] The Glossator is also loath to accept this canon in the sense that it departs from universal principles of law.[72]

(b) Subsidiary Methods of Proof

Various other possible ways of proving that a marriage had been contracted were suggested in a letter of Alexander III (1159–1181) to the Archbishop of Genoa. This letter was a cause of lengthy discussion among the decretal canonists who examined each one of its elements. The case concerned a certain free woman who, after having lived with a serf for ten years or more, denied that he was her husband inasmuch as there were no witnesses of their marriage. The serf claimed the contrary. In order to prove that they were married he introduced a document

---

[69] C. 1, X, *de clandestina desponsatione,* IV, 3; Comp. I, c. 2, *h.t.* (4, 3). (This canon is of uncertain origin. In the *Compilatio* I it is attributed by Friedberg to the Council of Agde [506].)

[70] *Summa Aurea,* Lib. IV, tit. *de clandestina desponsatione,* n. 6.

[71] *Commentaria,* Lib. IV, tit. *de clandestina desponsatione,* c. 1, nn. 1, 5.

[72] *Glossa Ord.* ad c. 1, X, *de clandestina desponsatione,* IV, 3, s. v. *casus.*

in which they were named husband and wife, and which showed that he had given her a *donatio propter nuptias.* The man also produced witnesses who had seen the woman wearing a ring. The Pope in his reply stated that in a doubt of this type the common repute (*fama*) of the neighborhood was to be the guiding norm. If the public opinion of the locality considered that the man had treated the woman as his wife, then they should be ordered to live together as husband and wife, especially if the aforesaid document had been drawn up by one who faithfully fulfilled his duty.[73]

The canonists discussed the probative value of the three elements mentioned in the Papal letter, that is, the *nominatio* or the fact that the couple called themselves spouses, the *tractatus* or the fact that a man treated a woman as his wife, and the *fama* or common repute.

The *nominatio* was of little importance since, as Panormitanus observed, those who were not married often claimed to be in order to conceal their crime.[74]

As a mode of proof cohabitation of itself was of no great value, as the decretal letter seems to indicate, but cohabitation joined with the *tractatus* was considered to constitute a strong probative agency. Panormitanus was of the persuasion that if the man and woman lived together and treated each other as man and wife and furthermore manifested before witnesses that they wished this to be an expression of their mutual exchange of conjugal rights, then this was to be taken as a full proof for the contraction of the marriage. Panormitanus [75] and Hostiensis [76] concurred in this opinion.

The *fama* or the public opinion was the element which the Papal letter particularly stressed. The Glossator also notes that it is to be taken into consideration when deciding such cases, but does

---

[73] C. 11, X, *de praesumptionibus,* II, 23; Comp. I, c. 14, *de sponsalibus et matrimoniis* (4, 1); Jaffé, n. 13969. (The exact date of this letter is uncertain.)

[74] *Commentaria,* Lib. II, tit. *de praesumptionibus,* c. XI, n. 8.

[75] *Commentaria,* Lib. II, tit. *de praesumptionibus,* c. XI, n. 7.

[76] *Commentaria,* Lib. II, tit. *de praesumptionibus,* c. XI, n. 9.

not concede full proof to it unless it be further supported by other adminicular proofs.[77]

A combination of these three elements assuredly formed full proof. Panormitanus seems clearly to assert this when he declares that cohabitation for a period of ten years, together with evidence that in the public mind a couple were considered to be man and wife and treated each other as such, constitutes complete proof of the contraction of marriage.[78] The doctrine on this section of the decretal is not clearly defined. It appears to have been proposed by the authors with some hesitation. Esmein († 1913) explains that the difficulty of the authors began when they endeavored to form a complete proof out of various combinations or single elements which, if considered alone, did not have full probative value.[79]

Two further possible proofs remain to be considered under this decretal—the *donatio propter nuptias* and the wedding ring. The *donatio propter nuptias* was a sum of money which the man was wont to give to his prospective bride. This custom prevailed among the Germanic nations.[80] This transaction was drawn up in documentary form and registered before a notary. The reply of the Pope in this case seems not to value such a document as anything more than a subsidiary proof, which when standing alone had no full probative value. Panormitanus and the Glossator support this view. Panormitanus gives as the reason the fact that this document was not primarily intended to prove the exchange of marital consent but to establish the bestowal of the gift.[81]

Finally, of what value in proving the contraction of her marriage was the wearing of the wedding ring by a woman? The proof by witness that a woman had been seen to wear a wedding ring at best could only establish a presumption in favor of her contraction of marriage. It was not regarded as full proof.

[77] *Glossa Ord.* ad c. 11, X, *de praesumptionibus,* II, 23, s. v. *fama loci.*

[78] *Commentaria,* Lib. II, *de praesumptionibus,* c. XI, n. 8.

[79] *Le Mariage En Droit Canonique,* I, 225.

[80] Cf. *Glossa Ord.* ad c. 31, C. XXVII, q. 2, s. v. *dotavit.*

[81] *Commentaria,* Lib. II, tit. *de praesumptionibus,* C. XI, n. 6; *Glossa Ord.* ad c. 11, *X, de praesumptionibus,* II, 23, s. v. *donationem.*

This answer is dictated by the decretal letter. The Pope did not consider it as a conclusive proof that the marriage had been contracted when the man proposed it as an argument in his favor.

Panormitanus treats the question in the following manner. If it could be established with certainty that in a locality only the married women wore rings, and single women were not permitted to wear them, then in a doubtful case the contraction of marriage could be presumed when a man and woman lived together and the woman wore a ring. If such a custom could not be shown to exist, the simple wearing of the ring was of no probative value.[82] If it could be shown that a man had given a ring to a woman the probative value of such testimony would be estimated again according to the custom prevalent in the locality. In some places the ring was given in connection with the celebration of marriage. Where such a usage obtained the bestowal of the ring could be regarded as a presumption which militated for the contraction of the marriage. In other places the ring was given in connection with the betrothal ceremony. Wherever this practice existed it could reasonably be presumed that it implied nothing more than the betrothal.[83]

The Glossator seems to qualify this somewhat when he says that the giving of the ring constitutes a presumption for the contraction of marriage only if it was given to the woman in church or at home.[84] Against these presumptions a contrary proof could always prevail.[85]

(c) Presumptive Marriage

The numerous clandestine marriages caused the law to recognize also a presumptive marriage, that is, in view of some objective fact the marriage was presumed to exist. When the conditions which formed the basis of the presumption were verified, then the law of the Decretals presumed that the parties intended this

---

[82] *Commentaria,* Lib. II, tit. *de praesumptionibus,* c. XI, n. 12.

[83] *Ibid.,* n. 12.

[84] *Glossa Ord.* ad c. 11, X, *de praesumptionibus,* II, 33, s. v. *annulos.*

[85] Panormitanus, *Commentaria,* Lib. II, tit. *de praesumptionibus,* c. XI, n. 12.

to be an expression of their marital consent. There were three types of these presumptive marriages:

(1) When a carnal union was consummated between validly betrothed persons;

(2) When a promise to marry was made conditionally and then, before the fulfillment of the condition, sexual intercourse took place between the betrothed parties; and

(3) When marriage was invalidly contracted because of a lack of the required age in one or both of the parties, then it was automatically validated if after the parties became of age they ratified it by sexual intercourse or in some other manner, by either word or fact.

The first type of presumptive marriage became the established law as a result of Gregory IX's (1227–1241) decision of a case as expressed in a letter to the Bishop of Le Mans. A betrothal was made between a man and a woman concerning their future marriage. Before their marriage took place sexual intercourse intervened. The man then contracted with a second woman a public marriage which he consummated. The Pope ruled that he had to return to the first woman, thereby implying the presumption that marriage had taken place between them. He stated further that no direct proof contrary to this presumption was admissible.[86]

The second type of presumption for the existence of marriage was recognized in a letter of Innocent III (1198–1216) to the Bishop of Marsico Nuovo.[87] The law presumed that in these circumstances the parties had abandoned the condition upon which they agreed. The Glossator appears to be of the conviction that this could be reduced to the first type of presumption in the case of *sponsalia de futuro* followed by carnal union.[88]

The third type of presumptive marriage was admitted in a

---

86 C. 30, X, *de sponsalibus et matrimonio,* IV, 1; Potthast, n. 9661. (This was written in 1227.)

87 C. 6, X, *de conditionibus appositis in desponsatione vel in aliis contractibus,* IV, 5; Comp. III, c. 1, *h.t.* (4, 4).

88 *Glossa Ord.* ad c. 6, *de conditionibus appositis in desponsatione vel in aliis contractibus,* IV, 5, s. v. *praesumendum.*

decree of Boniface VIII (1294–1303).[89] In this supposition the fact upon which the presumption rested could be not only the coition but also the fact that they called themselves husband and wife or lived together.[90]

What was the probative value of these presumptions for the existence of marriage? The Glossator and Panormitanus state clearly that the first presumption is a *praesumptio iuris et de iure,* although Panormitanus, contrary to Hostiensis, denies that it would be of binding force in the internal forum, if the carnal union with the first woman had not been accompanied by the *affectus maritalis.*[91] Panormitanus holds the same doctrine regarding the second type of presumptive marriage.[92] The exact nature of the third presumption is not so clearly expressed. Later commentators, however, have not hesitated to say that this also was a *praesumptio iuris et de iure.*[93]

---

[89] C. un., *de desponsatione impuberum,* IV, 2, in VI°.

[90] *Glossa Ord.* ad c. unic., *de desponsatione impuberum,* IV, 2, in VI° s. v. *modum alium.*

[91] *Glossa Ord.* ad c. 30, X, IV, 1; Panormitanus, *Commentaria,* Lib. IV, tit. *de sponsalibus et matrimonio,* nn. 1–2.

[92] *Commentaria,* Lib. IV, tit. *de conditionibus appositis,* c. XI, n. 2.

[93] Wernz, *Ius Decretalium,* IV, p. 29, n. 29, note 12; De Smet, *De Sponsalibus et Matrimonio,* n. 158, nota b.

CHAPTER III

From the Council of Trent to the Code of Canon Law

Article 1. Baptism

A. The Baptismal Register

It has been seen that in the law of the Papal Decretals there existed no universal custom of conserving records of baptism. Where such records were found to exist their authenticity was dubious. Consequently there was no authentic official document that one could produce in order to substantiate the fact of his baptism. The foundation of an agency whereby records of baptism were preserved and from which conclusive proof could be extracted is to be attributed to the Council of Trent. This agency took the form of a record to be maintained in the local parishes in which the pastor was to write the names of those whom he baptized and also the names of the sponsors. This measure was approved by the Council of Trent on November 11, 1563.[1]

The legislative demand of a written record of baptism was a most useful addition to the body of church law. Through it there was afforded a readily accessible means of proving that one had been baptized. It was also a preventive against the contracting of marriage by persons impeded from so doing by reason of the spiritual relationship arising from valid sponsorship at baptism.

B. The Probative Value Inherent in the Baptismal Register

Once the parochial record of baptism had been given its official status by the Council of Trent, canonists were quick to concede

---

[1] Conc. Trident., sess. XXIV, *de ref. matrim.*, c. 2—*Concilii Tridentini Diariorum, Actorum, Epistolarum, Tractatuum Nova Collectio* (ed. Societas Goerresiana, 13 vols., Friburgi Brisgoviae: B. Herder, 1901–1938), IX, 969; Mansi, XXXIII, 152–153.

to it full probative value in regard to what the record directly affirmed, namely, the reception of baptism.[2]

The parochial baptismal register, although not classed as a public document since it was not drawn up with legal formality, nevertheless furnished full proof of the fact which it reported. The record obtained this note of authenticity because of the fact that it was under the guardianship of the pastor. The burden of keeping such a record would have been uselessly imposed upon the pastor by the Council of Trent had the record not been recognized as entirely authentic. Hence the register enjoyed the presumption of veracity until such time that it could be proved to have been falsified.[3]

The jurisprudence of the time, however, recognized certain qualifications as necessary for the probative value of this record. It was considered to be a proof primarily only of the principal fact that it was intended to establish, that is, that baptism had been conferred. This fact was directly within the scope of the pastor's office. The record did not enjoy the same force if its use was extended to prove other facts outside the ambit of the pastoral office. It certified only to what was substantially connected with the administration of the sacrament, not to those things which were accidental to its administration.[4]

The baptismal record enjoyed the favor of the law, that is, it was presumed to be true. The truth of the record could, how-

---

[2] Schmalzgrueber († 1735), *Ius Ecclesiasticum Universum* (5 vols. in 12, Romae, 1843–1845), Lib. III, tit. 22, n. 47; Lucidi (fl. 1666), *De Visitatione Sacrorum Liminum* (3. ed., 3 vols., Romae, 1883), I, p. 398, n. 248; Reiffenstuel († 1703), *Ius Canonicum Universum* (6 vols., Romae, 1831–1834), Lib. II, tit. 22, n. 127; De Luca († 1683), *Theatrum Veritatis et Iustitiae* (16 vols., Coloniae Agrippinae, 1706), VII, disc. 30, n. 8; Monacelli (ca. 1714), *Formularium Legale Practicum Fori Ecclesiastici* (Venetiis, 1706), Tit. X, n. 2.

[3] Schmalzgrueber, *Ius Ecclesiasticum Universum,* Lib. II, tit. 22, n. 47; Reiffenstuel, *Ius Canonicum Universum,* Lib. II, tit. 22, n. 147.

[4] De Luca, *Theatrum Veritatis et Iustitiae,* Tom. VII, discurs. 30, n. 7; S. C. C., *Melevitana,* 30 dec. 1842—Pallottini, *Collectio Omnium Conclusionum et Resolutionum quae in causis propositis apud S. Cong. Cardinalium S. Concilii Tridentini Interpretum prodierunt ab anno 1564 ad annum 1860* (18 vols., Romae, 1868–1893), XIII, 457.

ever, be impugned on the basis that the record had been falsified or incorrectly annotated. To overthrow the evidently demonstrated testimony of the record contrary evidence had to be produced.[5] Thus the Sacred Congregation of the Council preferred to accept the evidence of a baptismal record certifying to a person's baptism rather than the testimony of the parent claiming that the pastor had only supplied the ceremonies of baptism and not actually administered the sacrament.[6] Therefore, unless the written attestation in the records was overthrown by the contrary testimony of a plurality of witnesses, the baptismal record offered conclusive proof.

C. *Post-Tridentine Legislation Concerning the Baptismal Register*

After its introduction by the Council of Trent, the prescription requiring the keeping of this register was soon assimilated into the laws of many provincial councils and synods. More particular instructions for its care were introduced, and the book was often made subject to the visitation of the bishop.[7]

The Roman Ritual of Paul V, published in 1614, gave detailed instructions concerning the annotations to be made in the bap-

---

[5] Devoti († 1820), *Institutionum Canonicarum Libri IV* (4. ed. Romana, Leodii, 1874), Lib. III, tit. 9, n. 21.

[6] S. C. C., *Brixien.*, 27 aug. 1796—*Thesaurus Resolutionum Sacrae Congregationis Concilii* (167 vols., Romae, 1718–1908), LXV, 209–220, 296; *Codicis Iuris Canonici Fontes cura Emi. Petri Card. Gasparri Editi* (9 vols., Romae: Typis Polyglottis Vaticanis, 1923–1939, Vols. VII, VIII, IX ed. *cura et studio Emi. Iustiniani Card. Serédi*), n. 3902 (henceforth this work will be cited *Fontes*).

[7] I Provincial Council of Milan (1565), Pars II, tit. 64, *quae pertinent ad baptismi administrationem*—Mansi, XXXIV, A, 16; IV Provincial Council of Milan (1576), Pars II, tit. 2, *quae pertinent ad sacramentum baptismi*—Mansi, XXXIV, A, 219; Provincial Council of Rouen (1581), *de sacramentis*, c. 5—Mansi, XXXIV, A, 623; Provincial Council of Tours (1583), Tit. VI, *de baptismo*—Mansi, XXXIV, A, 816; Provincial Council of Cambrai (1586), Tit. VI, *de sacramento baptismi*, c. 14—Mansi, XXXIV, B, 1235; Provincial Council of Toulouse (1590), Cap. II, *de baptismo*, c. 14— Mansi, XXXIV, B, 1285; Provincial Council of Malines (1607), Tit. III, cap. 2—Mansi, XXXIV, B, 1446; Provincial Council of Narbonne (1609), cap. XXXII—Mansi, XXXIV, B, 1513.

tismal register.[8] This work is notable because of the influence it had in making the use of the baptismal register become more widely diffused.

Pope Benedict XIV (1740–1758) in the year 1741 made special provision for proving the baptism of children born of a secret marriage (*matrimonium conscientiae*). Their baptism was not to be inscribed in the usual parochial book, but in a particular register to be kept in the archives of the episcopal chancery.[9] The Congregation of the Propagation of the Faith in an instruction of 1863, for certain grave reasons, permitted pastors to baptize children belonging to a different rite. A special book was commanded for the registration of such baptisms.[10] Since both of these records were prescribed by ecclesiastical authority, they enjoyed the same official status as the parochial record of baptisms. When invoked as proof of the reception of baptism, they constituted convincing proof.

Outside of the above-mentioned official records no other form of documentary evidence appears to have been accepted by the Church law as an unqualified proof that baptism had been administered. The worth of a private document was estimated according to the reliability of its author. Private documents certifying to the fact of baptism were generally not honored unless the author was known and he was thought to be above suspicion. Thus when foundling children were discovered with tags about their necks and upon the tags it was stated that they had been baptized, these notes were not considered sufficient proof that baptism had been received, and as a result conditional baptism was administered. The pastor was absolved from the obligation of conditionally baptizing such children only in the event that he

---

[8] *Rituale Romanum, Pauli V Pontificis Maximi iussu editum* (Antverpiae, 1614), Tit. XII, cap. 2.

[9] Benedictus XIV, ep. encycl., "*Satis vobis,*" 14 nov. 1741—*Fontes,* n. 319.

[10] S. C. de Propaganda Fide, instr., 6 oct. 1863—*Collectanea S. Congregationis de Propaganda Fide* (2 vols., Romae: Typographia Polyglotta S. C. de Propaganda Fide, 1907), n. 1243 (henceforth this work will be cited *Collectanea*) ; this document is also found in the *Fontes,* n. 4859.

could identify the person who had written the note and knew him to be a reliable witness.[11]

An instruction of the Holy Office in the year 1724 also advised conditional rebaptism in similar circumstances.[12] The Congregation of the Council also stated that conditional baptism of such foundlings could be omitted only if there was no doubt as to the reliability of the document certifying to their baptism.[13] The obvious intent of these laws was to care for the salvation of the child by removing all doubt as to whether or not it had been baptized.

D. *Testimonial Evidence*

The principles respecting proof that baptism had been administered, which are found in the *Decree* of Gratian, became a permanent part of ecclesiastical jurisprudence. Evidences of their application are to be found throughout the law after Trent. Proof established through the introduction of witnesses testifying that baptism had been received was still frequently used. When records of baptism had been destroyed or could not be obtained for some other reason, the proof by means of witnesses had to be utilized.

The question of what evidence was required to establish the reception of baptism was contingent upon the particular case at issue. If it was entirely a personal matter with no possible reference to the public good or to the interests of a third party, then little was exacted in the way of proof. If, however, proof of the reception of baptism was required as a qualification for the cor-

---

[11] Ferraris († ca. 1763), *Prompta Bibliotheca Canonica, Iuridica, Moralis, Theologica, necnon Ascetica, Polemica, Rubristica, Historica* (9 vols., Romae, 1885–1899), I, s. v. *Baptismus*, n. 62.

[12] S. C. S. Off., instr., 5 ian. 1724: "Si testimonium (de baptismo collato) sit ab homine incerto, in re adeo gravi, ignoto testimonio deferri non potest; quare tunc rebaptizandus est infans sub conditione, etiamsi schedulam de suscepto Baptismate a collo suspensam ferat, ut pro expositis utitur in locis quibusdam . . . "—*Collectanea*, n. 299; *Fontes*, n. 782.

[13] S. C. C., *Urbis*, 18 dec. 1723—*Thesaurus Resolutionum Sacrae Congregationis Concilii*, III, 2; *Fontes*, n. 3273; cf. Provincial Synod of Aix (1585) *de baptismi sacramento*—Mansi, XXXIV, B, 943.

rect performance of an act that would have effects extending beyond the private good of the individual himself, then stronger evidence had to be produced.

The fact of the reception of baptism could be established through the testimony of a plurality of witnesses. A number of witnesses proved this fact with absolute moral certitude.[14] This was the evidence which the law demanded. Relaxation of this requirement was not readily granted. Consequently when, because of grave danger to the life of a child, a midwife was permitted to baptize privately, she was commanded to obtain, if possible, two witnesses to the baptism.[15] The Congregation of the Propagation of the Faith in 1869 instructed missionaries to rebaptize conditionally persons who had been baptized by catechists, unless there had been present at the baptism two witnesses who could testify that the sacrament had been properly conferred.[16] These witnesses could testify both to the fact of the baptism and also as to whether or not the correct matter and form had been used.

In certain circumstances, however, if only one witness was available, his testimony constituted sufficient proof of the sacrament's reception.[17] This deviation from the general mode of procedure was justified only upon the fulfillment of certain stipulations regarding the question at issue and the person of the witness. The case had to be of such a nature as not to be prejudicial to the rights of another. If proof of one's reception of

---

[14] Benedictus XIV, *De Synodo Dioecesana* (4 vols., Lovanii, 1763), Lib. VII, cap. 6, n. 4; Provincial Council of Rheims (1583) *de baptismo*, c. 9—Mansi, XXXIV, A, 690.

[15] V Provincial Council of Milan (1579), Pars I, tit. 7, *quae ad baptismum pertinent*—Mansi, XXXIV, A, 362; Provincial Council of Aix (1585), *de baptismi sacramento*—Mansi, XXXIV, B, 945–946; Provincial Council of Narbonne (1609), Cap. XXXII—Mansi, XXXIV, B, 1513, *et passim*.

[16] S. C. de Prop. Fide, instr. (Ad Vic. Ap. Indiar. Orient.), 8 sept. 1869, n. 43, 2—*Collectanea*, n. 1346; *Fontes*, n. 4876.

[17] Mascardus († 1588), *Conclusiones Omnium Probationum Quae in Utroque Iure Quotidie Versantur* (3 vols., Venetiis, 1593), I, Conclus. 163, n. 1; Devoti, *Institutionum Canonicarum Libri IV*, Lib. III, tit. 9, n. 8; Benedictus XIV, *De Synodo Dioecesana*, Lib. VII, cap. 6, n. 4; Ferraris, *Bibliotheca*, I, s. v. *Baptismus*, n. 62.

baptism were a possible source of loss or damage to a third person, more extensive proof was demanded.[18]

The individual who acted as witness could be either a man or a woman. This witness, however, had to be one whose testimony was above all suspicion. If his or her testimony was suspected of deceit or falsehood, then the force of the testimony was vitiated and the fact of baptism was not established.[19] The testimony of a witness who was not "*omni exceptione maior*" was of no value. The force of the testimony of the witness was augmented if he himself had administered the sacrament and if he was endowed with such qualities as made his testimony credible.[20] Consequently a qualified witness, such as a pastor who by virtue of his office administered the sacrament, was always capable of substantiating the fact of baptism.[21]

Under certain conditions greater latitude in the matter of proof was permissible. The proof of the reception of baptism as a requirement for contracting marriage could be established equivalently by the production of an authentic testimony of confirmation or First Communion; at the hour of death the word of the parties themselves that they had been baptized was all that was required.[22]

---

[18] S. C. C., *Brixien.*, 11 febr. 1797—*Thesaurus Resolutionum Sacrae Congregationis Concilii,* LXVI, 27; *Fontes,* n. 3904; Mascardus, *op. cit.*, I; Conclus. 163, n. 5; Farinacius († 1618), *Tractatus de Testibus* (Venetiis, (1609), Quaest. LXIII, n. 26; Pirhing († 1679), *Jus Canonicum Nova Methodo Explicatum* (5 vols., Dilingae, 1674–1678), Lib. II, tit. 20, n. 112.

[19] Benedictus XIV, ep. "*Postremo mense,*" 28 febr. 1747, n. 31—*Fontes,* n. 377. This letter may also be found in the *Bullarium Benedicti XIV* (3 *vols. in* 4, *Prati,* 1845–1847), II, 170–191; S. C. de Prop. Fide, instr. (Ad Vic. Ap. Indiar. Orient.), 8 sept. 1869—*Fontes,* n. 4876; *Collectanea,* n. 1346; Lega, († 1935), *Praelectiones De Iudiciis Ecclesiasticis* (2 books in 4 vols., Romae, 1896–1901), I, 496.

[20] Benedictus XIV, ep. "*Postremo mense,*" 28 febr. 1747, n. 31—*loc. cit.*

[21] Pax Jordanus (fl. 1630), *Elucubrationes Diversae* (3 vols., Coloniae Allobrogum et Lugduni, 1729), Lib. XIV, tit. 20, n. 49; Devoti, *Institutionum Canonicarum Libri IV,* Lib. III, tit. 9, n. 8.

[22] Gasparri († 1934), *Tractatus Canonicus de Matrimonio* (2 vols., Parisiis, 1891–1892), n. 122.

ARTICLE 2. CONFIRMATION

A. The Confirmation Register

Shortly after the need of keeping a baptismal register was proclaimed by the Council of Trent, the practice of keeping a parochial record of the persons receiving confirmation appeared in the legislation of provincial councils and synods.[23] The Roman Ritual (1614) made it obligatory for pastors to keep a register of the confirmed.[24] From that time on the keeping of a register of the confirmed was a matter of universal law, and together with the parochial books this register was confided to the custody of the pastor. No other legitimate documentary proof of the reception of confirmation was introduced by law until the time of the present Code.[25]

B. The Probative Value Inherent in the Confirmation Register

This official record and also any authentic copies of it constituted the natural proof that one had received the sacrament of confirmation.[26] Evidence in documentary form was the most secure method of establishing the fact of the administration of this sacrament. Whenever obtainable this method of proof was preferable. In certain cases written proof was mandatory, if it could be conveniently secured. Thus for the reception of holy

---

[23] I Provincial Council of Milan (1565), Pars II, cap. 3—Mansi, XXXIV, A, 16–17; IV Provincial Council of Milan (1576), Pars III, tit. 3, *de visitatione*—Mansi, XXXIV, A, 287; Provincial Council of Aix (1585), *de confirmationis sacramento*—Mansi, XXXIV, B, 946; Provincial Council of Toulouse (1590), Cap. III, *de confirmatione*—Mansi, XXXIV, B, 1285; Provincial Council of Narbonne (1609), Cap. XV, *de confirmatione*—Mansi, XXXIV, B, 1493.

[24] *Rituale Romanum,* Tit. XII, cap. 1.

[25] For a detailed study of the post-Tridentine law on the keeping of parish records cf. O'Rourke, *Parish Registers,* The Catholic University of America Canon Law Studies, n. 88 (Washington, D. C.: The Catholic University of America, 1934), pp. 38–42.

[26] Lucidi (fl. 1666), *De Visitatione Sacrorum Liminum,* I, pp. 402–403, n. 259; Giraldi († 1775), *Animadversiones et Additamenta Ad Barbosam De Officio et Potestate Parochi* (Romae, 1774), Pars I, cap. 7, n. 21; Gasparri, *Tractatus Canonicus de Matrimonio,* I, n. 122, pp. 72–73.

orders or matrimony a certificate of one's confirmation had to be produced. Other forms of proof that one had been confirmed were acceptable only if the document of confirmation could not be located.[27]

C. Testimonial Evidence

In the matter of proving that one had been confirmed, other forms of proof were admissible when documents could not be located. Witnesses served to establish the required proof and, as in the case of baptism, frequently one witness sufficed, provided that he was a person judged worthy of credence.[28] The sponsor who had been present at the confirmation was mentioned as an apt witness. The law was not insistent upon two witnesses being produced. In default of other proof the affirmation of the person himself corroborated by oath was accepted as proof of the reception of confirmation.[29] The proof of the reception of confirmation as required for promotion to sacred orders could be established in this fashion, if no other proof was available.[30]

ARTICLE 3. HOLY EUCHARIST AND PENANCE

A. The Liber de Statu Animarum

These two sacraments may be treated together, for the sole particular occasion upon which the law demanded proof of their reception was in connection with the fulfillment of the precept of paschal communion and annual confession. The IV General Council of the Lateran (1215) introduced the law of annual confession and of communion during the Easter season for every Catholic who had attained the use of reason.[31] This law remained

---

[27] Gasparri, *op. cit.,* I, n. 121; Wernz's († 1914) view is somewhat milder in regard to the necessity of producing a document, cf. *Ius Decretalium,* IV, p. 188, n. 133.

[28] Farinacius, *De Testibus,* Quaest. LXIII, n. 26; Lega, *Praelectiones De Iudiciis Ecclesiasticis,* I, 496; Ferrairis, *Bibliotheca,* VII, s. v. *Testis,* n. 6.

[29] Wernz, *Ius Decretalium,* IV, p. 188, n. 133.

[30] Gasparri, *Tractatus Canonicus de Sacra Ordinatione* (2 vols., Parisiis, 1893–1894), n. 685.

[31] Can. 21: "Omnis utriusque sexus fidelis, postquam ad annos discretionis pervenerit, omnia sua solus peccata confiteatur fideliter, saltem semel in anno,

without substantial modification in the Decretals of Gregory IX,[32] and in the Council of Trent.[33]

Failure to comply with the demands of this law rendered one liable to severe penalties. He who failed in this duty was to be cut off from the Church in life and in death, *"et vivens ab ingressu ecclesiae arceatur, et moriens christiana careat sepultura."* Schroeder says that this was not a *latae sententiae* penalty. If, after being warned, the delinquent still refused to obey the law, the bishop could apply this penalty at his discretion. In the realm of the common law the penalty was of a *ferendae sententiae* character.[34]

To facilitate the practical observance of this law there was introduced the parochial record which is today called the *liber de statu animarum*. In its origin it was a tabulation, compiled by the pastor, of persons who complied with the law of annual confession and Easter communion in his parish. Mention of this record appeared in provincial conciliar and diocesan synodal legislation before that of any of the other parish books.[35] This record constituted a legitimate proof of one's reception of these two

---

proprio sacerdoti, et injunctam sibi poenitentiam studeat pro viribus adimplere, suscipiens reverenter ad minus in Pascha eucharistiae sacramentum; nisi forte de consilio proprii sacerdotis, ob aliquam rationabilem causam ad tempus ab ejus perceptione duxerit abstinendum; alioquin et vivens ab ingressu ecclesiae arceatur, et moriens christiana careat sepultura. Unde hoc salutare statutum frequenter in ecclesiis publicetur, ne quisquam ignorantiae caecitate velamen excusationis assumat. Si quis autem alieno sacerdoti voluerit justa de causa confiteri peccata, licentiam prius postulet et obtineat a proprio sacerdote, cum aliter ille ipse non possit solvere, vel ligare." Mansi, XXII, 1007–1010; Schroeder, *Disciplinary Decrees of the General Councils* (St. Louis, B. Herder Book Co., 1937), p. 570.

[32] C. 12, X, *de poenitentiis et remissionibus*, V, 38.

[33] Sessio XIII, *De eucharistia*, c. 9; sessio XIV, *De poenit. et extr. unct.* c. 5.

[34] Schroeder, *op. cit.*, pp. 262–263.

[35] Provincial Council of Narbonne (1227), Tit. VII—Mansi, XXIII, 23; Provincial Council of Béziers (1246), Cap. XLVI—Mansi, XXIII, 704; Provincial Council of Arles (1275), Cap. XIX—Mansi, XXIV, 152; Provincial Council of Bourges (1286), Cap. XIII—Mansi, XXIV, 631; Provincial Council of Salamanca (1335), Can. XLI—Mansi, XXV, 1146; *et passim.*

sacraments. It permitted the local pastor to testify to this effect if need for it arose.

B. Other Methods of Proof

The annual confession was to be made to one's own pastor, "*proprio sacerdoti,*" [36] or to a priest of one's choice with the pastor's permission. No statement was made in the law concerning the place where the paschal communion was to be received, but by custom it became general to fulfill this obligation in the parish church. This custom was approved by the Holy See.[37] Travelers (*peregrini*) and others who were unable to be at home during the period of the Easter season were permitted to fulfill these obligations in the particular parish in which they were at the time.[38]

For such persons there arose the need of proving these facts to the satisfaction of their proper pastor. Because of the penal sanction at that time contained in the law, documentary evidence was usually exacted as proof for the fulfillment of that law. Proof was furnished in the form of certificates testifying that the person had complied with the law of annual confession and communion. The practice of demanding these certificates in attestation of the reception of paschal communion is said to have originated in Rome. It was approved by local synods of the seventeenth century.[39] Confessional certificates were also commanded by synods and provincial councils.[40] The pastor was obliged to exact this proof from the travelers upon their return to his parish unless his knowledge of the person made such a query superfluous.[41]

---

[36] Many († 1922), *Praelectiones de Missa* (Parisiis, 1903), p. 306.

[37] Benedictus XIV, ep. encycl. "*Magno cum,*" 2 iun. 1751, nn. 21, 22—*Fontes,* n. 413.

[38] Giraldi, *De Officio et Potestate Parochi,* Pars II, cap. 19, n. 15.

[39] Cf. "De la Confession Annuelle et de la Communion Pascale"—*Analecta Iuris Pontificii,* IV (1860), cols. 2260–2290, esp. cols. 2274–2275.

[40] IV Provincial Council of Milan (1576), Pars II, cap. 5—Mansi, XXXIV, A, 228; Provincial Council of Aix (1585), *Quae ad poen. sacr. pertinent*—Mansi, XXXIV, B, 955; Provincial Council of Toulouse (1590), Pars II, cap. 4, c. 5—Mansi, XXXIV, B, 1286.

[41] Giraldi, *De Officio et Potestate Parochi,* Pars II, cap. 20, n. 23; Provincial Council of Bordeaux (1583), Tit. X—Mansi, XXXIV, A, 756, 757.

ARTICLE 4. HOLY ORDERS

A. Testimonial Letters

It has been seen that during the periods of Gratian and the Papal Decretals documentary evidence of the reception of holy orders was derived from testimonial letters (*litterae formatae, commendatitiae*) and letters of dismissal (*litterae dimissoriales*). This same procedure was continued in the Tridentine law. The significance of these terms, however, changed during this interval and became more clearly defined. The dimissorial letters no longer connoted a method of excardination, but implied merely a permission to confer orders without involving any change in diocese for the cleric. When a bishop for some reason was incapable of ordaining one who was subject to his jurisdiction, he would send the cleric to another bishop and at the same time grant that bishop permission to ordain this subject. Testimonial letters were those which testified to the cleric's integrity of character. They testified to a cleric's personal moral character, to his freedom from any impediment to ordination, to his studies and to the orders he had already received.[42]

The commendatory or testimonial letters were, therefore, legal substantiation, in documentary form, of the reception of orders. Their purpose was to certify to the candidate's worthiness and to prove that certain orders had already been conferred upon him.[43] They were used not only by minor clerics in relation to the orders received by them, but also by priests as a testimony of their ordination to the priesthood.[44]

The Council of Trent forbade any bishop to allow a traveling cleric to celebrate Mass or to administer the sacraments in his diocese unless the cleric had commendatory letters from his own Ordinary.[45] The testimonial letters received their status in law

---

[42] Cf. Reiffenstuel, *Ius Canonicum Universum,* Lib. I, tit. 11, nn. 111, 112, 113.

[43] Schmalzgrueber, *Ius Ecclesiasticum Universum,* Lib. I, tit. 22, nn. 2, 3; Reiffenstuel, *Ius Canonicum Universum,* Lib. I, tit. 11, n. 113.

[44] Schmalzgrueber, *loc. cit.*

[45] Conc. Trident., sess. XXIII, *de ref.,* c. 16.

from the authority of the bishop whose signature they bore. Consequently they were of no legal value unless they were accompanied with the signature and seal of the bishop who issued them.[46]

To enable bishops to grant these letters intelligently, records were kept in the episcopal curia of all ordinations both to minor and to major orders. Provincial councils introduced this practice shortly after the Council of Trent.[47]

B. *Other Methods of Proof*

Sometimes these testimonial letters could not be employed to furnish legitimate proof that one had received orders, e.g., if they were lost while the cleric was a great distance from his home diocese. What other means were at his disposal to establish the fact of his ordination? In such circumstances the canonists permitted him to employ subsidiary methods of proof.

Proof of one's ordination could be established through the introduction of witnesses who could testify to the fact of one's ordination or to the content of the missing testimonial letters.[48] Was the testimony of one witness alone ever sufficient evidence of the reception of orders? Authors admitted the possibility of this contingently upon the fulfillment of the accustomed conditions. The single witness had to be one in whom trust could be prudently placed and the case had to be one from which was absent all likelihood or ready possibility of prejudice to another's right. Consequently for the mere exercise of a priestly office, e.g., for the saying of Mass, one witness in support of the priest's ordina-

---

[46] Mascardus, *Conclusiones Omnium Probationum Quae in Utroque Iure Quotidie Versantur,* I, Conclus. 305, n. 2.

[47] I Provincial Council of Milan (1565), Pars II, cap. IX—Mansi, XXXIV, A, 25; Provincial Council of Benevento (1695), Tit. XV, cap. 3—*Acta et Decreta Sacrorum Conciliorum Recentiorum, Collectio Lacensis* (7 vols., Friburgi Brisgoviae: Herder, 1870–1890), I, 39 (hereafter this work will be cited as *Coll. Lac.*) ; Council of the Ruthenians, Greek Catholic Rite (1720), Tit. VIII—*Coll. Lac.,* II, 52; Provincial Council of Rome (1725), Appendix XI—*Coll. Lac.,* I, 422; Provincial Synod of Mount Lebanon (1736), Pars III, cap. 5—*Coll. Lac.* II, 330.

[48] Reiffenstuel, *Ius Canonicum Universum,* Lib. I, tit. 21, n. 5.

tion sufficed. In a judicial trial concerning the possession of a benefice more abundant testimony had to be advanced.[49]

Schmalzgrueber (1663–1735) observed that the formalities of proof were not demanded of one who came from a neighboring diocese and asked for permission to say Mass. The common practice was to exact such formal proof only from one who was unknown or who came from afar.[50]

ARTICLE 5. MATRIMONY

A. The Matrimonial Register

The Council of Trent treated several topics which are pertinent here. Among various modifications of the matrimonial discipline, the great reform Council, for the first time in the history of Canon law, prescribed the keeping of a parochial book for the recording of marriages.[51] By virtue of this decree the pastor was obliged to have a special book, of which he was to be the custodian, and in which a record was to be kept of the marriages celebrated in the parish. The pastor was to inscribe therein the names of the contracting parties, of the witnesses, the day and the place where the marriage took place. This prescription was part of the "*Tametsi*" decree on clandestine marriage. It was not contained in the original draft of the decree, nor in its first revision, but it was inserted in the second, third, and also the final revision. The decree gained conciliar approval in the twenty-fourth session of the Council held on November 11, 1563.[52]

The ancient law, as has been seen, failed to organize a specific proof relative to the fact of the celebration of a marriage. With the enactment of the Tridentine law there was required a partic-

---

[49] Farinacius, *De Testibus,* Quaest. LXIII, nn. 26, 28; Reiffenstuel, *Ius Canonicum Universum,* Lib. I, tit. 21, n. 7; Ferraris, *Bibliotheca,* VII, s. v. *Testis,* n. 6; Lega, *Praelectiones de Iudiciis Ecclesiasticis,* I, 496.

[50] *Ius Ecclesiasticum Universum,* Lib. I, tit. 22, n. 3.

[51] Conc. Trident., sess. XXIV, *de ref. matrim.,* c. 1: "Habeat parochus librum in quo conjugum et testium nomina diemque et locum contracti matrimonii describat quem apud se custodiat."—Mansi, XXXIII, 153.

[52] Cf. *Concilii Tridentini Diariorum, Actorum, Epistolarum, Tractatuum Nova Collectio,* IX, 640, 683, 762, 890, 969.

ular and adequate proof that marriage had been contracted.[53] That this was the purpose of the Council in passing such a measure may be gathered from an examination of the earlier forms of the decree. The second revision of the decree had this further addition to the law governing the matrimonial register, "*et ei (libro) fides in probandis matrimoniis adhibeatur.*" [54] Many disputes were thus provided against and the fact of the celebration of a marriage was thus made clearly available to ecclesiastical authority. This law contributed greatly to obviating much of the confusion attendant upon the proof of the celebration of a marriage, which confusion had existed under the old law.

B. *The Probative Value Inherent in the Matrimonial Register*

The parish matrimonial record was recognized as furnishing complete proof of the existence of a marriage and consequently was acknowledged as worthy of entire credence. It was constituted in this capacity by public authority and was entrusted to the custody of the pastor as part of the duties of his office. The matrimonial register enjoyed the same authenticity as a public document and could be impugned only on the grounds that it had been in some manner falsified. This opinion was shared generally among canonists.[55]

The same probative value was granted to certificates drawn up from the records in the marriage book. In regard to certificates Lucidi (fl. 1666) and Gasparri (1852–1934) further stipulated that they could be accepted in trials only on the condition that they were faithful reproductions of the record itself, that is, the exact wording of the record had to be used on the certificate.[56]

It is to be noted that before the Code of Canon Law the matri-

---

[53] Esmein, *Le Mariage En Droit Canonique*, II, 214.

[54] *Concilii Tridentini Diariorum Actorum Epistolarum Tractatuum Nova Collectio*, IX, 762.

[55] Schmalzgrueber, *Ius Ecclesiasticum Universum*, Lib. III, tit. 22, n. 47; Lucidi, *De Visitatione Sacrorum Liminum*, I, p. 398, n. 248; Wernz, *Ius Decretalium*, V, p. 316, n. 197; Reiffenstuel, *Ius Canonicum Universum*, Lib. II, tit. 22, n. 127; Esmein, *Le Mariage En Droit Canonique*, II, 214.

[56] Lucidi, *De Visitatione Sacrorum Liminum*, I, p. 398, n. 248; Gasparri, *Tractatus Canonicus de Matrimonio*, II, p. 216, n. 1052.

monial register was not designated as a public instrument as it is in the present law.[57] This, however, did not in any way detract from its authenticity. A public document was one drawn up by a notary with due solemnity.[58] Other documents were private. Certain private documents, nevertheless, were recognized as being authentic, and hence enjoyed the status of public instruments, even though they were not drawn up with all the formalities of a public instrument. The matrimonial register pertained to this class of documents. It was a private authentic instrument endowed with the same presumption of authority as a public instrument.[59]

The matrimonial register obtained this note of authenticity since it was composed by the pastor, lawfully deputed to do so, who testified concerning a matter coming within the scope of his office.[60] Neither the countersignature of a notary or of witnesses nor any further legal formality was required in order that the matrimonial register might be accepted as being endowed with full probative force.[61]

C. *Post-Tridentine Legislation Concerning the Matrimonial Register*

The Tridentine law on the matrimonial register was quickly put into practice by its assimilation into the decrees of many provincial Councils and synods. The pastor's duty of carefully conserving these records was stressed, and frequently the book was made subject to episcopal visitation.[62]

---

[57] Cf. Canon 1813, §1, n. 4.

[58] C. 2, X, *de fide instrumentorum,* II, 22.

[59] Schmalzgrueber, *Ius Ecclesiasticum Universum,* Lib. III, tit. 22, nn. 36–47.

[60] Giraldi, *Animadversiones et Additamenta Ad Barbosam De Officio et Potestate Parochi,* Pars I, cap. 7, n. 7.

[61] Sanchez († 1610), *De Sancto Matrimonio Disputationum Libri Decem in Tres Tomos Distributi* (3 vols., Antverpiae, 1626), Tomus I, Liber III, disputatio 15, n. 22; Pax Jordanus (fl. 1630), *Elucubrationes Diversae,* Liber III, tit. 7, n. 157.

[62] I Provincial Council of Milan (1565), Pars I, tit. 64, *Quae ad sacramentum Matrimonii pertinent*—Mansi, XXXIV, A, 71; IV Provincial Council of Milan (1576), Pars III, tit. 3, *De Visitatione*—Mansi, XXXIV, A, 287;

The Roman Ritual of Paul V, published in 1614, gave explicit directions for the annotations to be made in the parish matrimonial register. It named this book as one of the five which were to be in the possession of all those whose duty it was to administer the sacraments.[63] The influence of this work is easily discernible from the vast conciliar legislation which followed in the wake of its ordinances.[64] Many of these councils made specific reference to the prescription of the Ritual as well as to the legislation of the Council of Trent.

D. *Other Forms of Documentary Evidence*

In the year 1741 Benedict XIV in his encyclical letter "*Satis vobis*"[65] proposed the norms governing the celebration of the

Council of Bordeaux (1583), Tit. XV, *De Sacramento Matrimonii,* and Tit. XVIII, *De Parochis*—Mansi, XXXIV, A, 762 and 768; Provincial Council of Cambrai (1586), Tit. XI, *De sacramento matrimonii*—Mansi, XXXIV, B, 1240; Provincial Council of Avignon (1594), Tit. XLII, *De officio parochi*—Mansi, XXXIV, B, 1354; Provincial Council of Salerno (1596), Cap. XXII, *De Parochis*—Mansi, XXXV, B, 1008; Provincial Maronite Council (1596), c. 34—Mansi, XXXV, B, 1025; Council of San Severino (1597), Tit. *De sacramento matrimonii*—Mansi XXXV, B, 1050; Provincial Council of Amalfi (1597), Tit. *De sacramento matrimonii,* c. 3—Mansi, XXXV, B, 1120; Synod of Diamper (1599), Tit. *De sacramento matrimonii,* Decertum IV—Mansi, XXXV, B, 1300; Council of Narbonne (1609), Cap. XXXII—Mansi, XXXIV, B, 1513; *et passim.*

[63] *Rituale Romanum, Pauli V Pontificis Maximi iussu editum,* Tit. XII, cap. 4.

[64] Provincial Synod of Benevento (1693), Cap. XVI—*Coll. Lac.,* I, 72; Provincial Synod of Naples (1699), Tit. III, cap. 9, *De sacramento matrimonii,* n. 11—*Coll. Lac.,* I, 180; Provincial Council of Albano (1703), Pars II, Tit. *De sacramento matrimonii*—*Coll. Lac.,* I, 309; Provincial Council of Embrun (1727), cap. V, *De parochis,* c. 7—*Coll. Lac.,* I, 626; Synod of Mount Lebanon (1736), Pars II, cap. 11, *De sacramento matrimonii*—*Coll. Lac.,* II, 178; Provincial Council of Bordeaux (1850), Tit. III, cap. 7, *De matrimonio,* n. 6—*Coll. Lac.,* IV, 575; Provincial Council of Toulouse (1850), Tit. III, cap. 1, *De matrimonio,* c. 78—*Coll. Lac.,* IV, 1055; Provincial Council of Auch (1851), Tit. III, cap. 1, 7, *De matrimonio,* c. 106—*Coll. Lac.,* IV, 1191; Provincial Council of Prague (1860), Tit. IV, cap. 11, *De sacramento matrimonii*—*Coll. Lac.,* V, 519; Provincial Council of Colombia, S. A. (1868), Tit. II, cap. 7, *De parochis*—*Coll. Lac.,* VI, 481, and others.

[65] Benedictus XIV, ep. encycl., "*Satis vobis,*" 14 nov. 1741—*Fontes,* n. 319,

secret marriage (*matrimonium conscientiae*). He made provision for the proof of the contraction of such a marriage by introducing a new type of register. This register was to be used exclusively for the inscription of secret marriages and was to be preserved in the episcopal chancery. The Pontiff left no doubt as to what juridical value was to be attached to attestations of the celebration of marriage taken from this register. He directed that they merit the same assurance as was generally conceded to the parochial registers of baptism and marriage.[66]

In the matter of documentary evidence a final recourse for the proof of the celebration of marriage was added by the "*Ne temere*" decree issued by the Congregation of the Council in the year 1907. This decree ordered the celebration of a marriage to be registered not only in the usual marriage book but also in the baptismal register. If one party had been baptized elsewhere, then the pastor of the parish where the marriage took place was to notify the pastor of the parish where the baptism had been conferred. The pastor of the place of baptism then had to note the marriage in his baptismal record.[67] This annotation in the baptismal record furnished of course an added documentary proof of the celebration of marriage.[68]

E. *Testimonial Evidence*

The Council of Trent introduced a new method for proving the existence of a marital union. This legislation, however, in no way derogated from the value of other proofs which were previously in use. Nothing in the law of the Council could be construed to that effect. The Council simply added another resource without wishing to suppress the old ones.[69] The registration of the marriage was not an essential condition of the proof of its

[66] 14: ". . . tantam promereri fidem, quantam sibi alii libri parochiales baptismatis et matrimonii vindicare consueverunt . . ."—*Fontes*, n. 319.

[67] S. C. C., decr. "*Ne temere,*" 2 aug. 1907, art. IX, 2—*Acta Sanctae Sedis* (41 vols., Romae, 1865–1908), XL (1907), 529. (This series will be quoted hereafter as *ASS*). This document is also cited in the *Fontes,* n. 4340.

[68] Wernz-Vidal, *Ius Canonicum,* V, n. 580.

[69] Esmein, *Le Mariage En Droit Canonique,* II, 214.

celebration.[70] If documentary proof was not used, either because the documents had been destroyed or because they were not easily obtainable, other methods of proof had to be utilized. These subsidiary methods of proof became more clearly defined after the Council of Trent. The question of the method to be selected depended upon the manner in which the marriage had been celebrated.

(a) Public Marriage

The Council of Trent prescribed as a condition of validity that marriage be celebrated in the presence of the pastor, or of the priest delegated by the pastor or the Ordinary, and two or three witnesses.[71] When the parties complied with this prescription there was ample testimonial evidence of the existence of the marriage. Navarrus (Martinus de Azpilcueta, 1496-1583)[72] and Leurenius (1646-1723)[73] stated that the principal reason for which the Council required the presence of witnesses at the marriage was for the matter of having available proof of the celebration of the marriage.

The celebration of the marriage could be proved, first of all, by the united testimony of the assisting priest and witnesses.[74] The same effect, namely full proof of the contraction of a marriage, was obtained by the testimony of the witnesses alone.[75]

The Congregation of the Council in the year 1684 described the procedure for proving the existence of a marriage by means of witnesses when the record of the celebration of the marriage could not be found in the marriage register. The parties were first required to affirm under oath the existence of their marriage.

---

[70] Pallottini, *Collectio Omnium Conclusionum et Resolutionum,* XIII, 457.

[71] Sessio XXIV, *de ref. matrim.,* c. 1.

[72] *Consilia seu Responsa* (6 vols., Venetiis, 1621), Lib. IV, Consilium 11, E.

[73] *Forum Ecclesiasticum* (5 vols., Venetiis, 1729), Lib. IV, tit. 3, quaest. 153, n. 3.

[74] S. C. C., *Theatina,* 22 nov. 1856—Pallottini, *Collectio Omnium Conclusionum et Resolutionum,* XII, 484.

[75] De Luca (1614-1683), *Theatrum Veritatis et Iustitiae,* Tom. III, Pars II, Disc. VI, n. 2; Bangen (1823-1865), *Instructio Practica de Sponsalibus et Matrimonio* (3 titles in 1 vol., Monasterii, 1858-1860), Tit. III, p. 71.

Then the testimony of the witnesses who had been present at the marriage celebration had to be secured. After this the pastor was free to register the marriage in the book of marriages.[76] The Congregation of the Council [77] and the Rota [78] have accepted the testimony of witnesses alone as a convincing proof of the celebration of marriage.

That the testimony of witnesses testifying to the celebration of a marriage might be accepted as conclusive, it was only necessary that they be able to affirm the mutual exchange of consent before the pastor. The canonists therefore concluded that they could not fulfill the office of witness unless they were cognizant of what was taking place and perceived either by sight or hearing the exchange of consent.[79] For only under these conditions could a person afterwards say that he had witnessed the marriage being contracted. The deposition of witnesses who claimed to have been present at the marriage ceremony was however subject to rebuttal if the opponent could show that actually they had not been in attendance at the marriage ceremony.[80]

Finally, the testimony of the pastor as a qualified witness to the ceremony was sufficient proof.[81] One of the canonists, nevertheless, wished the pastor's testimony to be further supported by adminicular proofs, if no record of the marriage could be found.[82] The celebration of a public marriage, therefore, could be established by testimonial evidence on the part of the officiating pastor or delegated priest and witnesses, or by the testimony of the witnesses alone, or of the pastor alone.

---

[76] This decree is not contained in the sources available to the writer. It is partly quoted by Bangen, *op. cit.*, Tit. III, p. 73.

[77] S. C. C. *Florentina,* 10 sept. 1853, 28 ian., 18 mart., 29 iul. 1854—Pallottini, *op. cit.*, XIII, 460; the case is reported also in the *Fontes,* nn. 4134, 4139.

[78] S. R. Rota, *Decisiones Recentiores* (19 parts in 25 vols., Francofurti-Aureliae-Romae, 1623–1703), Pars XI, n. 3, decis. 395.

[79] Navarrus, *Consilia,* Lib. IV, Cons. 11, D; Sanchez, *De Sancto Matrimonio Disputationum Libri Decem,* Lib. III, disp. 41, n. 2.

[80] S. R. Rota, decis. 634 *coram Buratto, Florentina,* 27 ian. 1855—Pallottini, *Collectio Omnium Conclusionum et Resolutionum,* XIII, 225.

[81] De Luca, *Theatrum Veritatis et Iustitiae,* Tom. III, disc. 6.

[82] Pax Jordanus, *Elucubrationes Diversae,* Lib. XIV, tit. 20, n. 49.

(b) Clandestine Marriage

Due to the lack of the universal promulgation of the Tridentine law which invalidated marriage when it was celebrated outside the juridical form, many regions remained immune to the "*Tametsi*" decree. In those regions, then, where the law of the Council of Trent was not promulgated, it was still possible validly to contract a clandestine marriage.[83] Thus the later commentators on the Decretals again enunciated the principles taken from the Decretal law for evaluating the proof of the existence of a clandestine union. These principles after the Council of Trent became distinctly outlined and were generally acknowledged by canonists. Since they were substantially the law which existed prior to the Council of Trent, it will be sufficient to consider them in a summary fashion.

(1) The denial by both parties of the existence of a marital union established its non-existence, provided that no proof of the contracting of the marriage was available.[84]

(2) When one party affirmed the existence of the marriage and the other denied it, the burden of proof rested with the party who claimed that the marriage had been contracted. Upon failure to prove such a contention the law did not prevent the parties from entering another union.[85]

(3) The acknowledgment by both parties that they had contracted clandestinely served to establish the existence of the marriage, when other proofs were lacking.[86]

The last mentioned rule suffered a notable exception. The dual confession of the celebration of a clandestine marriage did not

[83] The term "clandestine" is here used to signify a marriage contracted without the required presence of priest and witnesses. Cf. Carrière († 1864), *Praelectiones de Matrimonio* (2 vols., Paris, 1837), I, p. 401, n. 1173; Leurenius († 1723), *Forum Ecclesiasticum,* Lib. IV, tit. 3, quaest. 143.

[84] Pirhing († 1679), *Ius Canonicum Nova Methodo Explicatum,* Lib. IV, tit. 3, n. 2; Schmalzgrueber († 1735), *Ius Ecclesiasticum Universum,* Lib. IV, tit. 3, n. 249.

[85] Schmalzgrueber, *op. cit.,* Lib. IV, tit. 3, n. 248; Fagnanus († 1678), *Ius Canonicum seu Commentaria Absolutissima in Quinque Libros Decretalium* (5 vols., Venetiis, 1696), Lib. IV, *de cland. desp.,* cap. 1, n. 5.

[86] Schmalzgrueber, *op. cit.,* Lib. IV, tit. 3, n. 248; Pirhing, *op. cit.,* Lib. IV, tit. 3, n. 34.

prejudice a later public marriage entered into by one of the parties. The contraction of the clandestine marriage had to be further proved in some other way or it had to be shown that the public marriage had been invalidly contracted because of some diriment impediment. If neither of these two alternatives could be utilized, then the public marriage was favored by the law as a valid union.[87]

The reason for this decision was not that the public marriage dissolved the clandestine one, but that the ecclesiastical judge had to pronounce as valid the public marriage duly proved rather than the clandestine marriage possibly valid in God's sight, but minus the proof sufficient to establish its validity. The evidence at hand was of necessity the guiding norm for an ecclesiastical judge.[88]

A later response of the Congregation of the Sacraments on March 6, 1911, confirmed the rule regarding the dual affirmation of the parties as well as the exception to it. The Congregation was asked if the simple affirmation of the parties could be accepted as an adequate proof of the existence of their marriage when other proofs were lacking. The Congregation replied that the usual proofs should first be diligently sought. In the event that after such investigation proof was not obtainable, the parties had to affirm under oath the fact of their marriage, before they were considered as lawfully united in marriage and their children regarded as legitimate. Those cases, however, wherein the law required full proof had to be excepted, namely, when there was question of prejudice to another marriage or of the receiving of the sacrament of orders.[89]

This response provided a measure to be utilized only in extreme cases when all other proofs were lacking. Only in these circumstances could the acknowledgment of the parties themselves constitute a proof of the celebration of their marriage. This measure served a useful purpose for proving the existence of a marriage

[87] Schmalzgrueber, *op. cit.*, Lib. IV, tit. 3, nn. 251–252; Pirhing, *op. cit.*, Lib. IV, tit. 3, n. 34; Fagnanus, *op. cit.*, Lib. IV, tit. *de cland. desp.* 17, 7.

[88] Schmalzgrueber, *op. cit.*, Lib. IV, tit. 3, n. 252; Pirhing, *op. cit.*, Lib. IV, tit. 3, n. 35; Wernz, *Ius Decretalium*, V, p. 300, n. 188.

[89] *Acta Apostolicae Sedis, Commentarium Officiale* (Romae, 1909–), III (1911), 103. (Henceforth this collection will be cited as *AAS*.)

contracted in foreign countries whenever documentary proof could not be readily obtained.

(c) Presumptive Marriage

It has been seen that in certain specific instances, under the law of the Papal Decretals, the existence of a presumptive marriage was acknowldeged. The "*Tametsi*" decree of the Council of Trent, and also the "*Ne temere*" decree which required a formal contraction of marriage by Catholics who prepared to enter a marital union, made such a presumption of the existence of a marriage impossible. From the time of the Council of Trent, therefore, the presumptive marriage was outlawed in all regions where the Tridentine decree was promulgated or observed by custom. When the Tridentine form became a condition of valid consent, there could no longer be any possibility of consent being equivalently manifested through sexual intercourse.[90] All three types of presumptive marriage—the carnally consummated union between validly betrothed persons, the carnally consummated union between prospectively betrothed persons prior to the fulfillment of the condition attaching to their betrothal, and the carnally consummated union between persons of canonical age when their earlier contraction of marriage was invalid because of the impediment of nonage—then disappeared from canonical practice.

In the regions, however, which remained unaffected by the Tridentine law on the form for contracting marriage these presumptive marriages were not abrogated. Pope Leo XIII in his decree "*Consensus mutuus*" ultimately abolished the presumptive marriage—which was based upon the betrothal followed by sexual union—for the territories where an informal marriage could otherwise still have been validly contracted.[91] This decree made no specific mention of the two other types of presumptive marriage, namely, the case of a conditional promise to marry followed by a carnal union, and the validation by word or fact of a marriage invalid through a lack of the requisite age. They,

---

[90] Sanchez, *De Sancto Matrimonio Disputationum Libri Decem*, Lib. III, disp. 40, n. 3.

[91] Leo XIII, decr. "*Consensus mutuus*," 15 febr. 1592—*Fontes*, n. 613.

therefore, retained their force of inevitable presumptions until the promulgation of the present Code.

Consequent to the Council of Trent, then, the most widely used method of proving that marriage had been contracted was that which looked to the matrimonial record preserved at the parish where the marriage had taken place. The testimonial proof was less generally used, for it was more difficult.[92] Its application seems to have been confined to occasions when the written record had been destroyed or was obtainable only with great difficulty.

---

[92] Bangen, *Instructio Practica de Sponsalibus et Matrimonio,* Tit. III, p. 71.

PART TWO

CANONICAL COMMENTARY

CHAPTER IV

Baptism

ARTICLE 1. DOCUMENTARY EVIDENCE

A. The Baptismal Register

The principal agency which the Code of Canon Law provides as a means for proving the fact of baptism is the parochial record of baptisms or the baptismal register. The aim of the law in this regard is to have preserved in an official book a permanent and authentic record of every administration of the sacrament of baptism. The baptismal register is parochial in character, being enumerated among other parish records which are entrusted to the care and supervision of the pastor. His is the obligation of maintaining this register.[1]

If the register is to be a true index of events that have taken place, and therefore a trustworthy source of evidence, it must be carefully and accurately annotated. Consequently the pastor is obliged to see that the baptismal register is kept in an orderly fashion.[2] The baptismal register, as the law itself makes clear, should be in book form. As a consequence, the practice of keeping these records on separate sheets of paper or on cards, which might easily be mislaid, is not only not recommendable, but also

---

1 "Habeat parochus libros paroeciales, idest librum baptizatorum . . ."—Canon 470, §1.

2 ". . . et omnes hos libros, secundum usum ab Ecclesia probatum vel a proprio Ordinario praescriptum, conscribat ac diligenter asservet."—Canon 470, §1.

not permissible.[3] The baptismal register is, therefore, an authoritative tabulation which certifies to the administration of baptism and the identity of those baptized.

B. *The Registration of Baptism*

In order that everyone may have available a public record of his baptism, the Code takes appropriate measures to insure that a proper registration be made of the baptism in whatever circumstances it may have been administered.

The maintenance of parochial records is the personal obligation of the pastor. The Code continually mentions the pastor as the one obliged to care for the registration of the various sacraments.[4] When there has been negligence in regard to the matter either of maintaining the records or of making the necessary entries therein, the pastor is the one liable to such penalties as the Ordinary may judge to be proportionate to the gravity of the offense.[5] The pastor, therefore, is charged with the task of registering the baptisms which are conferred in his parish. The registration to be made consists of the notation of the name of the person baptized, together with the names of his parents and sponsors as well as of the minister, and of the recording of the day and place of the baptism.[6] Because of the important juridical effects resulting from baptism, and in view of the necessity of having the record for the use of the person baptized, the pastor's obligation of making a careful entry of the baptism is a grave one.[7] When the

---

[3] Vermeersch, *Theologia Moralis* (3. ed., 4 vols., Romae: Università Gregoriana, 1933), III, n. 237; Sipos, *Enchiridion Iuris Canonici* (3. ed., Pecs: "Ex Typographia Haladas R. T.," 1936), p. 322.

[4] Cf. canons 470, §1; 777, §1; 798, §1; 1103.

[5] Canon 2406, §1.

[6] Canon 777, §1. A discussion of the manner of registration may be found in O'Rourke, *Parish Registers,* The Catholic University of America Canon Law Studies, n. 88 (Washington, D. C.: The Catholic University of America, 1934). Instructions on the registration of the names of illegitimate children are given by McDevitt, *Legitimacy and Legitimation,* The Catholic University of America Canon Law Studies, n. 138 (Washington, D. C.: The Catholic University of America Press, 1941).

[7] Vermeersch, *Theologia Moralis,* III, n. 237; Cappello, *Tractatus Canonico-Moralis de Sacramentis* (3 vols, in 6, Taurinorum Augustae: Marietti,

pastor is ill or absent, the duty of registering the baptism devolves upon the priest in charge of the parish or on the priest who administered the sacrament.[8]

There is a quite general custom of confiding the matter of registration to the assistant pastor or curate. In virtue of the common law this is neither the right nor the duty of the assistant. This duty is incumbent upon the pastor, who is responsible for the registration even though he does not confer the sacrament himself. Authors, however, do not condemn the practice of permitting assistants to sign the register.[9] The source of the assistant's rights and duties is threefold, namely, the statutes of the diocese, the Ordinary's letter of appointment and the pastor's commission.[10] The assistant may be delegated to register baptisms through any one of these three sources. Cappello [11] and Ayrinhac († 1930)[12] contend that the obligation of caring for the baptismal registration is so personal to the pastor that he may not habitually delegate it to another without a reasonable cause. Other authors, however, do not make this limitation. De Meester allows the assistant to presume the pastor's permission if no other explicit provision has been made.[13]

Delegation to lay people, however, does not seem justifiable.

1932–1939. Vol. I, 3. ed., 1938; Vol. II, Pars I, 3. ed., 1938; Vol. II, Pars II, 1932; Vol. II, Pars III, 1935; Vol. III, Pars I et II, 4. ed., 1939), III, n. 237 (this work will hereafter be referred to as *De Sacramentis*); Davis, *Moral and Pastoral Theology* (3. ed., 4 vols., New York: Sheed and Ward, 1938), III, 67.

[8] Murphy, "Parish Records"—*The American Ecclesiastical Review* (Philadelphia, 1889–1943; Baltimore, 1944–), LXV (1921), 3.

[9] Cappello, *De Sacramentis,* I, n. 188; De Smet († 1927), *Tractatus Dogmatico-Moralis De Sacramentis* (2. ed., Brugis: Car. Beyaert, 1927), n. 353; Davis, *Moral and Pastoral Theology,* III, 67; Waldron, *The Minister of Baptism,* The Catholic University of America Canon Law Studies, n. 170 (Washington, D. C.: The Catholic University of America Press, 1942), p. 172.

[10] Canon 476, §6.

[11] *De Sacramentis,* I, n. 188.

[12] *Legislation on the Sacraments* (New York—London: Longmans, Green and Co., 1928), p. 60.

[13] *Juris Canonici et Juris Canonico-Civilis Compendium* (nova editio, 3 vols. in 4, Brugis, 1921–1928), II, n. 887.

The Code itself warns against allowing the parochial records to fall into the hands of extraneous persons.[14] In view of this it would be contrary to the law to entrust the care of baptismal records to lay people.[15] When a priest other than the pastor annotates the register, the pastor should examine the register and add his countersignature. This provision is not laid down by the Code, but it is recommended by canonists.[16] The absence of the pastor's countersignature, however, does not invalidate the entry as a credible public record.

If the sacrament is not conferred by the proper pastor, and he is not present when it is administered, the minister of the sacrament must bring this fact to the attention of the proper pastor as soon as possible.[17] A private response of the Sacred Congregation of the Council directs that in this case the registration of the baptism should be made in the parish of its actual administration, and that the local pastor should also notify the pastor of the parish where the person baptized or his parents retain a domicile.[18] Neither by force of the canon nor in consequence of the above response would the domiciliary pastor be obliged to enter this baptism in his own register. It has been suggested, however, that he keep some record of the baptism, by noting it either in the *liber de statu animarum*,[19] or in his own baptismal record,[20] or in a special book maintained for this purpose.[21]

---

[14] Canon 470, §4.

[15] De Smet, *Tractatus Dogmatico-Moralis De Sacramentis*, n. 353; Cappello, *De Sacramentis*, I, n. 188.

[16] Vermeersch-Creusen, *Epitome Iuris Canonici* (3 vols., Mechliniae-Romae: H. Dessain, 1934–1937. Vol. I, 6. ed., 1937; Vol. II, 5. ed., 1934; Vol. III, 5. ed., 1936), II, n. 55; Davis, *Moral and Pastoral Theology*, III, 67; Cappello, *De Sacramentis*, I, n. 188.

[17] Canon 778.

[18] This response, given on January 31, 1927, may be found in Bouscaren, *Canon Law Digest* (2 vols., Milwaukee: Bruce Publishing Co., Vol. I, 1934, Vol. II, 1943), II, 184.

[19] Sipos, *Enchiridion Iuris Canonici*, p. 448.

[20] Beste, *Introductio in Codicem* (Collegeville, Minn.: St. John's Abbey Press, 1938), p. 483.

[21] *The Irish Ecclesiastical Record* (Dublin, 1864–), 5th Series, XXXV (1930), 417.

This point has been most recently treated by the Congregation of the Sacraments in its latest instruction on the investigation to be made by the pastor before assisting at marriage. This Instruction recommends that the Ordinary take the necessary steps to see that a baptism conferred possibly outside the parish of origin shall be properly registered in both the register of the church where the baptism was performed and also in the register of the place of origin. Wherefore, the pastor or rector of the church where the baptism is conferred shall as soon as possible transmit to the rector of the parish of origin a written report covering faithfully each and every element that is required by law (Canon 777) for the completion of the record of baptism.[22] If this provision is observed, then the record of baptism will be more readily accessible by reason of its being kept in two different registers. This apparently is the reason for the ruling of the Congregation on this point.

A lay person baptizing privately in case of necessity would be bound by canon 778 to notify the domiciliary pastor of the person baptized.[23] Basing his opinion on the above mentioned response of the Congregation of the Council, Waldron states that it would be sufficient to notify the local pastor, who could then bring this fact to the attention of the domiciliary pastor.[24] This would seem to be a safe procedure, since the response would dictate, in these circumstances, that the baptism be recorded in the register of the parish of actual administration. In view of the Instruction of the Congregation of the Sacraments referred to previously, the local pastor should then send a report of the baptism to the pastor of the parish of origin of the person baptized.

The baptism of children born of secret marriages (*matrimonium conscientiae*) is not to be inscribed in the general parochial register, but in a special register maintained for this purpose in the archives of the diocesan curia. The parents of the child are

---

[22] S. C. de Sacramentis, instr., 29 iun. 1941, n. 11, d—*AAS*, XXXIII (1941), 306. This Instruction may also be found in Bouscaren, *Canon Law Digest*, II, 253–276.

[23] Cappello, *De Sacramentis*, I, n. 188.

[24] *The Minister of Baptism*, p. 173; cf. Fanfani, *De Iure Parochorum* (2. ed., Romae: Marietti, 1929), p. 223.

obliged to notify the bishop of the baptism either personally or by letter.[25]

It may happen that mistakes will occur in making the registration of the baptism. If these are discovered at a later date, may the pastor make the necessary changes? Cappello prohibits this unless the pastor has first referred the matter to the Ordinary.[26] Bouuaert-Simenon allow the pastor to make whatever corrections are necessary unless the matter is sufficiently grave to warrant that the Ordinary's approbation be sought before changing an entry already made. Thus if the correction to be made touches upon the question of legitimacy they advise a prior consultation with the Ordinary.[27] The latter view seems to offer the more logical opinion. If accuracy demands that certain changes be made, the lawfully appointed custodian of the register should be competent to make them in most cases. Prudence suggests that the pastor verify the facts before making any corrections. This could easily be done by interrogating the parents or the sponsors of the child baptized.

C. *Baptismal Certificates and Copies*

Two other public documents are commonly invoked to substantiate the reception of baptism, namely baptismal certificates and copies of the baptismal record.[28] Both of these documents are written transcripts taken from the original baptismal record. A certificate (*attestatio scripta*) relates merely the sense or the facts of primary import shown on the baptismal record. A copy (*exemplar authenticum*) is a literal reproduction of the first document, that is, it narrates all the items entered in the original record.[29] Some of the older authors were of the opinion that

[25] Benedictus XIV, ep. encycl., "*Satis vobis,*" 14 nov. 1741—*Fontes,* n. 319; cf. De Smet, *Tractatus Dogmatico-Moralis De Sacramentis,* n. 355.

[26] *De Sacramentis,* I, n. 179.

[27] *Manuale Juris Canonici* (3 vols., Gandae et Leodii: Apud Auctores, 1930–1931. Vol. I, 3. ed., 1930; Vol. II, 1931; Vol. III, 3. ed., 1931), II, n. 57.

[28] Canon 1813, §1, n. 4.

[29] Coronata, *Institutiones Iuris Canonici* (5 vols., Romae: Marietti, 1933–1939. Vols. I et II, 2. ed., 1939; Vol. III, 1933; Vol. IV, 1935; Vol. V, 1936), III, n. 1342.

all copies of the baptismal register had to be filled out in the precise wording of the original.[30] At the present time, however, copies made of the baptismal register generally consist of mere excerpts of the original. They are printed on blank forms and testify that the records of the parish show that the person named was baptized in the parish on a given date. These certificates when properly drawn up and attested by signature and seal constitute authentic copies even though they are not reproductions made verbatim from the actual register.[31]

Canon Law makes no mention of the employment of photostatic copies of documents. Such a reproduction of a baptismal or other parish register, however, if made under the supervision of the pastor and accompanied by his letter of explanation and assurance concerning the copy, appears to merit the same credence as an authentic written transcript.

The term "authentic" or "to authenticate," when applied to documents, signifies a proper observance of the legal solemnities in the issuance of the document. A document is said to be authentic when a public official in the form prescribed by law attests that the said document is in conformity with the original.[32] Documents of parochial origin are rendered authentic by the signature of the pastor together with the seal of the parish.[33] In order to obtain this quality of authenticity, the common law does not require that a parochial document be also submitted to

---

[30] E.g., Giraldi († 1775), *Animadversiones et Additamenta Ad Barbosam De Officio et Potestate Parochi*, Pars I, cap. 7, n. 21.

[31] Cappello, *De Sacramentis*, I, n. 190; Wanenmacher, *Canonical Evidence in Marriage Cases* (Philadelphia: Dolphin Press, 1935), p. 208.

[32] Augustine († 1943), *A Commentary on the New Code of Canon Law* (8 vols., St. Louis: B. Herder Book Co., 1925–1938. Vol. I, 6. ed., 1931; Vol. II, 6. ed., 1936; Vol. III, 5. ed., 1938; Vol. IV, 3. ed., 1925; Vol. V, 5. ed., 1935; Vol. VI, 3. ed., 1931; Vol. VII, 3. ed., 1930; Vol. VIII, 3. ed., 1931), VII, 255; Vermeersch-Creusen, *Epitome Iuris Canonici*, III, n. 199; Noval († 1938), *Commentarium Codicis Iuris Canonici, Lib. IV, De Processibus*, 2 vols., Pars I, *De Iudiciis* (Romae: Marietti, 1920), n. 545. This volume of Augustine's work will henceforth be cited as *Ecclesiastical Trials*, and the work of Noval will be cited as *De Iudiciis*.

[33] Coronata, *Institutiones Iuris Canonici*, III, n. 1345.

the Ordinary for his approval. The document is authentic even though it is not stamped with the seal of the episcopal curia.[34]

The Instruction of the Congregation of the Sacraments issued on June 29, 1941, however, directs that when a baptismal certificate is transferred to another parish outside the diocese, the transmission is to be made through the local curia.[35] A diocesan statute or an episcopal decree may also demand that the transfer of a certificate to another diocese be accomplished through the intervention of the local Ordinary.[36]

The question which immediately comes to mind is one of competence. Whom does the law recognize as competent to issue or to authenticate these certificates of baptism? The wording of the Code partially solves this question by denoting ordinaries, pastors and ecclesiastical notaries as persons capable of authenticating these documents.[37]

The word "*parochus*" appears to comprehend all those who function with parochial power, or all those to whom the law entrusts the duties and prerogatives of a pastor. Such persons are the *quasi-parochus,* the *vicarius paroecialis* if endowed with full parochial rights,[38] e.g., the acting vicar when a parish is *pleno iure* united to a religious house,[39] the administrator (*vicarius oeconomus*) for the interval during which a parish is without a pastor,[40] the *vicarius substitutus* constituted according to canon 465, §4 [41] and the parochial adjutant who assumes all the functions of the pastor.[42] By reason of the fact that the incumbents of these offices during their tenure of office take the pastor's place and assume his responsibilities they are competent to issue certificates of baptism.[43]

---

[34] Cappello, *De Sacramentis,* I, n. 190.

[35] N. 4, a—*AAS,* XXXIII (1941), 299; Bouscaren, *Canon Law Digest,* II, 255.

[36] Cappello, *loc. cit.*

[37] Canon 1813, §1, n. 4.

[38] Canon 451, §2, nn. 1 and 2.

[39] Canon 471, §4.

[40] Canon 473, §1.

[41] Cf. canon 474.

[42] Canon 475, §2.

[43] Coronata, *Institutiones Iuris Canonici,* III, n. 1342.

The capacity of an assistant pastor in this matter is not so easily determined. If the question be considered solely under the aspect of the common law, it seems that the assistant in intrinsic relation to his assigned work has no power to authenticate parish documents. In no place does the law clearly attribute this right to him. There is, however, a more fundamental reason which indicates why the curate is not, in his own right, competent in this regard. That is the fact that the assistant is not generally considered to possess a canonical office in the strict acceptance of that term.[44] The baptismal certificate is a public document which may be drawn up only by one who is designated as a public official. If one denies that an assistant holds a strict canonical office, it is logical also to deny that the assistant is a public official in this matter, or recognized as such by the law. It seems likely, therefore, that in virtue of the common law alone the assistant pastor has no power to issue these certificates.[45] Cappello[46] and Coronata,[47] who treat this question explicitly, in the opinion of the writer do not contradict Augustine. When conceding this power to the parochial assistants of the pastor, they appear to contemplate a situation in which the assistant is taking the place of or substituting for the pastor, and hence acting with parochial power. Augustine also concedes that an assistant who takes the pastor's place (e.g., during a vacation) could issue these certificates, for in these circumstances the assistant becomes a *locum tenens*.[48] The essential concept of the assistant, however, is rather that of one who assists and works with the pastor.

The discussion is theoretical and not, therefore, a condemnation of the general custom which permits assistants to issue these certificates. The necessary power may certainly be delegated to them by diocesan statute, in the Ordinary's letter of appointment, or through the commission of the pastor. Furthermore, such

---

[44] Cf. canon 145, §1.

[45] Cf. Augustine, *Ecclesiastical Trials*, p. 257; Wanenmacher, *Canonical Evidence in Marriage Cases*, p. 208.

[46] *De Sacramentis*, I, n. 190.

[47] *Institutiones Iuris Canonici*, III, n. 1342.

[48] *Loc. cit.*

delegation may be presumed if no other provision has been made.[49] These sources of possible delegation offer a practical solution of the question.

D. The Probative Value Inherent in Public Documents Certifying the Reception of Baptism

The inscriptions of baptism which are contained in parochial baptismal registers as well as authentic copies and certificates taken from this register are classified as public ecclesiastical documents.[50] As public documents they are presumed genuine,[51] and consequently furnish full proof of those facts which are directly and primarily stated in them.[52] The assurance of fact inherent in these documents is sufficient to enable a judge to pronounce sentence with the moral certitude necessary for that act.[53] The probative value which is attributed to these documents is founded upon the presumption of their genuineness. This quality, when predicated of a document, signifies that the document was composed by the person reputed to be its author and that the facts which it relates really occurred.[54] It is a guarantee both of the document's authorship and of the truth of its content. This presumption of genuineness is a reasonable one in view of the character of the person who composes the document. The pastor is a public official, who by reason of his office is qualified to administer the sacrament of baptism and to care for its reliable registration. Consequently his public acknowledgment of the administration of the sacrament as recorded in official documents merits entire credibility.

A public document is one in which an official, with the correct observance of the requisite legal formality, relates an act which was executed by him or in his presence. The question arises as to how the record in a baptismal register fulfills this definition

[49] Augustine, *loc. cit.;* Wanenmacher, *op. cit.*, p. 208.

[50] Canon 1813, §1, n. 4.

[51] Canon 1814.

[52] Canon 1816.

[53] Noval, *De Iudiciis,* n. 545.

[54] Roberti, *De Processibus* (2 vols., Romae: Apud Aedes Facultatis Iuridicae ad S. Apollinaris, 1926), II, n. 370.

when it is annotated by one who indeed witnessed the act, but who is not legally recognized as a public person, or when the entry is made by one who is a public person, but who neither witnessed nor performed the act. Willett explains this difficulty by saying that, since the registers are in the hands of public persons whose duty it is to see that only what is true is entered in them, they, therefore, should be rightfully considered public documents.[55]

Another possible explanation of this difficulty appears, if one considers the status of the person who actually administers the sacrament or makes the baptismal entry. When an assistant pastor signs the register, after receiving lawful permission to do so, although he is not a public official by right of office, he nevertheless seems to be such in virtue of his delegation. Provided that he is correctly delegated to administer the sacrament and make the required entry in the register, he is acting as a public official. True, he is not a public official in virtue of any ordinary power coming to him from the common law. It is obvious, however, that the same effect may be obtained by one who functions with delegated authority as by one who acts with power inherent in the office he possesses. The pastor is not forbidden to allow another priest to register the baptism. When he commissions the assistant to care for this matter, or when diocesan statute gives the assistant that right, the latter is then a lawfully delegated official. So also, if the pastor should make the registration when an assistant or some other priest has administered the sacrament, he will include in this entry the name of the minister. Upon the authority of the one delegated to administer the sacrament could rest the evidence that the ceremony took place, because again he would appear to be an authorized public official in virtue of his delegation to administer the sacrament.

The reception of baptism is a public fact which is most securely and most naturally proved by the evidence of a public document. Whenever possible, therefore, this form of proof is the most desirable. The law qualifies the probative value of these public

---

[55] *The Probative Value of Documents in Ecclesiastical Trials,* The Catholic University of America Canon Law Studies, n. 171 (Washington, D. C.: The Catholic University of America Press, 1942), p. 55.

documents in a certain respect. The probative force of all public documents is restricted to those things which are directly and primarily affirmed in them.[56] The facts directly and primarily affirmed are those which are defined in the document and for the attesting of which the document was drawn up. In general, the register is proof only of those things which took place in the presence of the one who composed the document, for concerning these alone is he capable of testifying.[57]

The baptismal register, therefore, gives complete assurance regarding the fact that baptism was conferred upon the person named, regarding the identity of the sponsors and the minister, and regarding the date and place of the administered baptism. Other information which may be contained in the register, such as the parents' names or their domiciles, is subsidiary, and as a result is not fully proved by its appearance in the baptismal register. It must be said, however, that the entry in the register gives rise to a strong presumption of truth, even though it is not absolute proof of accessory information.[58] It is also to be noted that from the mere baptismal record it cannot be concluded that the sacrament was validly conferred. The register proves only that the external celebration or baptismal ceremony has taken place.[59]

It has been mentioned that the law calls for the registration of baptism to be made in a book kept for this purpose, and not on individual pieces of paper. Of what value as proof would be a baptismal entry made on a separate piece of paper and not in the register itself? It seems that so long as the annotation made on a separate piece of paper is in some way connected with the reg-

---

[56] "Documenta publica fidem faciunt de iis quae directe et principaliter in eisdem affirmantur."—Canon 1816.

[57] Coronata, *Institutiones Iuris Canonici,* III, n. 1347; Noval, *De Iudiciis,* n. 550; De Meester, *Juris Canonici et Juris Canonico-Civilis Compendium,* II, n. 859.

[58] S. R. Rota, *Nullitas matrimonii,* 14 mart. 1927, *coram R.P.D. Francisco Parrillo,* dec. XI, n. 8—*S. Romanae Rotae Decisiones seu Sententiae* (Romae, 1912–), XIX (1927), 75; S. R. Rota, *Nullitas matrimonii,* 8 iul. 1918, *coram R.P.D. Seraphino Many,* dec. X, n. 8—*Decisiones,* X (1918), 83.

[59] Coronata, *Institutiones Iuris Canonici,* III, n. 1347; Augustine, *Ecclesiastical Trials,* p. 260.

ister, it retains the value of a public document. If it is inserted in the register, it may still be regarded as a public document and a satisfactory form of evidence, provided that there is no doubt in regard to its genuineness.[60]

E. *Private Documents*

In the great majority of cases legitimate and public proof of the fact of baptism will be available through the registration of the baptism in the records of some parish church. It is possible, however, that the proof of one's baptism would have to depend upon the evidence of a private document, because no public record could be secured.

A private document is understood to be a writing composed by a private individual, or by a public person acting in a purely private capacity.[61] For example, a letter may be extant in which the writer states that he witnessed a certain baptism, or perhaps that he administered the sacrament himself. A pastor may have written a personal letter in which he mentions that he baptized a child known to the recipient of the letter. Documents issued by heretical or schismatical sects as well as the recording of baptisms in the family bible also pertain to this class of documents. Frequently proof of one's baptism will have to be based on them, since no other proof is obtainable. For this reason their worth in substantiating the reception of baptism shall have to be considered.

Documents which are purely private in nature can also be introduced as proof of the reception of baptism, in the event that evidence based on public records cannot be had. If the said document is examined by a competent person and accepted as genuine, the evidence which it affords can constitute a safe proof of the fact of baptism.[62] An example of this may be found in a Rota decision of the year 1911. A letter of one of the parties was

[60] Noval, *De Iudiciis*, n. 545; Wanenmacher, *Canonical Evidence in Marriage Cases*, p. 211.

[61] Augustine, *Ecclesiastical Trials*, p. 254.

[62] Cappello, *De Sacramentis*, III, n. 420; Muniz, *Procedimientos Eclesiásticos* (2. ed., 3 vols., Sevilla: Lib. de Sobrino de Izquierdo, 1926), II, n. 204.

introduced in which the writer declared that she had no knowledge of the church where she had been baptized. From this declaration made in the letter the court concluded that the lady took it for granted that she had been baptized and was doubtful only concerning the place of baptism. The evidence gathered from this private document was considered by the court to be a strong indication that the baptism had taken place.[63]

All private documents lack the initial legal presumption of genuineness possessed by public documents both as regards authorship and credibility.[64] As a result they should not be immediately received at face value. In order that a letter or any private document may be accepted as proof, the one who introduces it must show that the document is not a forgery and that its author is a reliable witness whose testimony can be believed. In other words, both the authorship of the document as well as the credibility of its content must be established. The authorship may be shown by having the writer acknowledge the document himself, or by producing witnesses who can testify that the letter was really written by the one who is believed to have done so. The writing could also be compared with other letters of which it is unmistakably known that they were written by the same person.[65] From this it can be seen that ultimately the value of any private document is to be estimated according to the knowledge and reliability of its author.

A document intended to be a public one, but not drawn up by the proper official, or destitute of a necessary legal formality, loses its character of a public document, because its authenticity is thereby destroyed. An example of this would be a baptismal certificate which has not been properly signed or which has not been stamped with the parish seal. Documents of this kind because of dubious authenticity do not possess the probative value attached to a correctly authenticated public document. In line of proof, therefore, they are classed as private documents. Because

---

[63] S. R. Rota, *Nullitas matrimonii,* 13 iun. 1911, *coram R.P.D. Francisco Heiner,* dec. XXIV, n. 9—*Decisiones,* III (1911), 262.

[64] Willett, *The Probative Value of Documents in Ecclesiastical Trials,* p. 90.

[65] Willett, *loc. cit.*

of defective compositor these documents cannot be considered as public documents, but they can serve as instruments of proof with the probative value accredited to a private document.[66] The one whose duty it would be to pass judgment on a document of this type would first have to take measures to establish the necessary authenticity of the document.

Documents of non-Catholic churches certifying to the reception of baptism are often presented to ecclesiastical authorities on the occasion of marriage or conversion. Of what value are these documents in proving the fact of baptism? Cappello states that documents emanating from non-Catholic sects cannot be received in the Church as a full proof of the reception of baptism.[67] The reason for this seems to be that from such documents no presumption that the sacrament was validly administered can be inferred. The certificate is no guarantee of correct practice.[68] A baptismal certificate from a non-Catholic sect is not, therefore, in and of itself a full proof of the reception of baptism. In an Instruction of the year 1883, the Sacred Congregation of the Propagation of the Faith attributed merely extrajudicial value to documents of heretical sects.[69] They would in virtue of this have only the probative value attaching to private documents. This appears to be the proper manner in which to treat these documents. Thus Cappello advises that the circumstances of the individual case be considered. The bishop shall be the final judge of the probative efficacy of any such non-Catholic baptismal certificate.[70]

For the reason that such certificates are frequently the only proof obtainable, they are accepted as proof when they may be believed genuine and credible, or if they be supported with further evidence confirmatory of the asserted baptism.[71] In the decision of the Rota on June 13, 1911, referred to previously, a declara-

---

[66] Coronata, *De Processibus,* n. 1344; S. R. Rota, *Iurispatronatus,* 22 nov. 1913, *coram R.P.D. Michaele Lega,* dec. XLIX, n. 13—*Decisiones,* V (1913), 594.

[67] *De Sacramentis,* I, n. 190.

[68] Davis, *Moral and Pastoral Theology,* III, 69.

[69] S. C. de Prop. Fide, instr., 1883, n. 33—*Fontes,* n. 4901.

[70] *De Sacramentis,* I, n. 190.

[71] Wanenmacher, *Canonical Evidence in Marriage Cases,* p. 233.

tion of nullity was sought for a marriage. It was alleged that the marriage was invalid because of the impediment of disparity of cult. The question of establishing the baptism of the lady, an Episcopalian, became the principal point at issue. Further substantiating evidence of her baptism was produced in the form of a record of baptism taken from the files of an Episcopalian church. The Rota designated this document as an ***argumentum gravius*** for the fact of baptism. When supported by corroborative evidence, the baptismal record of the non-Catholic sect was accepted as the definitive factor pointing to the probability of the lady's baptism.[72]

ARTICLE 2. SUBSIDIARY METHODS OF PROOF

A. The Necessity of Other Methods of Proof

Public documentary evidence to substantiate the fact of baptism is sometimes impossible to locate, either because the parochial records have been destroyed, or the church of one's baptism is unknown. At times a baptismal certificate can be secured only with great difficulty and after lengthy investigation for which there is not sufficient time. For these and other reasons the Code of Canon Law wisely recognizes other agencies of proof which may be utilized to prove the reception of baptism. Since the reception of baptism is a public fact, it also admits of proof by means of testimonial evidence. The introduction of witnesses who can testify to the baptism in question is an efficacious method of establishing the fact of baptism. The first possible witness to be considered is the one who is authorized by the law of the Church to give testimony certifying to the fact of baptism.

B. The Testimony of the Qualified Witness of Baptism

An authorized or qualified witness is a public official who is designated by law to testify to those acts which he executes or witnesses in the performance of the duties of his office.[73] In

[72] S. R. Rota, *Nullitas matrimonii,* 13 iun. 1911, *coram R.P.D. Francisco Heiner,* dec. XXIV, n. 10—*Decisiones,* III (1911), 262-263.

[73] Wernz-Vidal, *Ius Canonicum,* VI, n. 483; Noval, *De Iudiciis,* n. 512; Augustine, *Ecclesiastical Trials,* p. 239.

regard to the question of certifying to the fact of baptism, the pastor is the lawfully constituted authorized witness (*testis qualificatus*), provided that he conferred the sacrament himself or was present at its administration.[74]

The law itself estimates the value to be placed upon the testimony of a qualified witness. A qualified witness is capable of giving full proof concerning those acts which he performs *ex officio.*[75] The lawgiver reasonably presumes both accuracy and veracity in the deposition of an official who is appointed to that office with the end in view that he may be able to testify publicly to the administration of the important sacrament of baptism. The evidence attaching to the testimony of a qualified witness supplies the defect of other witnesses and is therefore equivalent in probative value to the testimony of two witnesses. When the pastor, as a qualified witness, testifies in favor of a baptism received, his testimony provides complete assurance of the sacrament's reception.[76] Moreover, since the pastor's testimony constitutes a full legal proof, it is decisive evidence whether or not the baptism is contested by another. Even in the event that another's right should be involved in the claim to baptism, the baptism would be adequately proved if substantiated by the testimony of a qualified witness.[77]

Muniz states that if the baptism is not recorded in the baptismal register, the pastor is still a trustworthy witness whose testimony must be believed. He says, however, that if there is no written record of the baptism the pastor's testimony alone would not be sufficient proof if there were danger of prejudice to another arising from the fact of baptism. He advances as his

---

[74] Ayrinhac, *Legislation on the Sacraments,* p. 61; Davis, *Moral and Pastoral Theology,* III, 68; S. R. Rota, *Nullitas matrimonii,* 24 febr. 1911, *coram R.P.D. Iosepho Mori,* dec. X, n. 12—*Decisiones,* III (1911), 101.

[75] Canon 1791, §1.

[76] Ayrinhac, *Legislation on the Sacraments,* p. 61; Cappello, *De Sacramentis,* III, n. 420; Davis, *Moral and Pastoral Theology,* III, 68; S. R. Rota, *Nullitas matrimonii,* 25 febr. 1911, *coram R.P.D. Iosepho Mori,* dec. X, n. 12—*Decisiones,* III (1911), 101.

[77] Ayrinhac, *Legislation on the Sacraments,* p. 61; Cappello, *De Sacramentis,* I, n. 189.

reason for this statement the fact that the doubt about the baptism is augmented by the pastor's failure to make a proper registration of the sacrament.[78] It seems that in this respect Muniz confuses two different forms of proof—documentary and testimonial. When a pastor bases his testimony on an existing record of baptism, his evidence is primarily documentary; when he testifies in virtue of his own recollection of the baptism, his testimony appears to be no less convincing. These two types of proof are distinct, and testimonial evidence is not necessarily dependent upon documents for its efficacy. So long as the matter pertains to his office of pastor, he is competent to testify as a qualified witness. This point was emphasized by the Roman Rota in a decision of the year 1911.[79]

A parallel may be drawn from another case of the Rota. A pastor had neglected to note in the marriage register that a dispensation from the impediment of disparity of worship had been secured for the celebration of a marriage. The validity of the marriage was later impugned on the score that no dispensation had been granted. The pastor testified that the required dispensation had been obtained, and that he had made no mention of it, since the notice of it was readily obtainable from the records of the Curia. The court declared that the pastor's deposition supplied the deficiency of the marriage record. It further stated that the interested parties should not be held liable for the pastor's negligence.[80] The testimony of the pastor, who is the qualified witness of baptism, is therefore always capable of supplementing a missing baptismal record.

The pastor is usually designated as the authorized witness of baptism. His testimony, for that reason, is accepted as a full legal proof. One naturally wonders if this same juridical value may be attributed to the testimony of an assistant pastor, or of a lawfully deputed priest or deacon, who has baptized the person whose baptism must be established. To solve this question it is

[78] *Procedimientos Eclesiásticos,* II, n. 204.

[79] S. R. Rota, *Nullitas matrimonii,* 28 aug. 1911, *coram R.P.D. Aloysio Sincero,* dec. XXXIX, n. 22—*Decisiones,* III (1911), 440–441.

[80] S. R. Rota, *Nullitas matrimonii,* 30 iun. 1910, *coram R. P. D. Michaele Lega,* dec. XXIII, n. 19—*Decisiones,* II (1910), p. 235.

necessary to know why the pastor is the authorized witness of baptism. A decision of the Rota has declared that the pastor is the *testis qualificatus* by reason of the fact that he is the ordinary minister of the sacrament of baptism.[81]

If this be the reason for the pastor's being an authorized witness, it would seem logical to infer that another cleric who takes the pastor's place in administering the sacrament would assume the pastor's right to testify to the baptism. In other words, the minister of solemn baptism in virtue of his authorization to administer the sacrament is also thereby qualified to testify to that fact. His testimony would then be equivalent to that of the pastor if the latter had administered the sacrament himself. If this were not the case, the authorized priest or deacon would be only a trustworthy witness whose testimony of itself would not constitute a full proof of the fact of baptism, if the rights of another were affected by the claim concerning the baptism.[82] Sipos seems to favor this view, for he designates the authorized witness of baptism as the *sacerdos baptizans.*[83]

C. *The Testimony of Other Witnesses*

When baptism is conferred, besides the minister and the recipient of the sacrament, there will generally be other persons also present. The sponsor or sponsors have a necessary function in the ceremony attendant upon the solemn administration of baptism.[84] If it can be conveniently accomplished, a sponsor should also be present at a baptism privately conferred. If this is not possible, a sponsor should be in attendance when the ceremonies of baptism are supplied.[85]

In addition to the godparents, the parents and relatives of the child baptized will often come to see the ceremony take place. Should necessity require it, all such persons could furnish testimony adequate to confirm the reception of baptism. The evi-

[81] S. R. Rota, *Nullitas matrimonii,* 25 febr. 1911, *coram R.P.D. Iosepho Mori,* dec. X, n. 12—*Decisiones,* III (1911), 101.

[82] Canon 779.

[83] *Enchiridion Iuris Canonici,* p. 448.

[84] Canon 762, §1.

[85] Canon 762, §2.

dence inherent in the testimony of those who were present when the sacrament was administered sufficiently determines one's reception of this sacrament.[86] When two or more witnesses can be summoned who are capable of testifying that the baptism has taken place, their testimony constitutes a full legal proof of the fact of baptism.[87] Since the evidence based on the testimony of a plurality of witnesses is a full legal proof, it would be decisive even though the fact of baptism were contested.

Authors suggest the godparents as particularly suitable witnesses of the baptism which must be proved.[88] Because of their active function in the ceremony of baptism, the godparents are likely to recall clearly the fact and circumstances of the baptism. For this reason their testimony will be of great worth in proving that the baptism has been conferred. The testimony of brothers and sisters of the person whose baptism is in doubt is also of great value. When the brothers and sisters seek to prove that the person was baptized in infancy, it is necessary that such brothers and sisters should have been at least seven years old at the time of the alleged baptism. That is, they must have enjoyed the use of reason at the time the baptism to which they testify took place.[89]

When the age of puberty has been attained, however, which is required in order that one may be a fit witness,[90] persons may testify to events which took place before they reached that age. The testimony of brothers and sisters, therefore, may not be rejected on the score that, because of lack of age, they were not capable witnesses at the time of baptism. The Rota has frequently enunciated the principle that persons who have attained the age of puberty may testify to what they observed before reaching that age, provided that the event took place after the witness attained the use of his reason.[91]

---

[86] Cappello, *De Sacramentis,* III, n. 509; Sipos, *Enchiridion Iuris Canonici,* p. 448.

[87] Canon 1791, §2.

[88] Gasparri, *Tractatus Canonicus de Matrimonio* (ed. nova ad mentem Codicis I. C., 2 vols., Typis Polyglottis Vaticanis, 1932), I, n. 141; De Smet, *De Sponsalibus et Matrimonio,* n. 678.

[89] Wanenmacher, *Canonical Evidence in Marriage Cases,* p. 121.

[90] Canon 1757, §1.

[91] S. R. Rota, *Nullitas matrimonii,* 29 iun. 1923, *coram R.P.D. Josepho*

When baptism is privately administered the Code directs that whenever possible two witnesses or at least one be used, by whom the administration of baptism may later be proved.[92] The legislative demand of witnesses at private baptism is a precautionary measure. It is hoped that in this way all doubt may be removed concerning the fact of baptism and its valid administration. When the aforesaid witnesses testify to the fact of the baptism, they should also be questioned about the matter and form used in the conferring of the sacrament.[93]

The witnesses referred to in this canon are to be distinguished from the godparents. The witnesses are called *testes* while the godparents are designated *patrini.*[94] The same individual could be both godparent and witness, provided of course that he possessed the qualifications for valid and licit sponsorship.[95] By reason of the Code's distinction, however, it may be rightly inferred that the qualities required for sponsorship need not be fulfilled in order that one may be a lawful witness. One incapable of being a valid or licit sponsor could be a witness, inasmuch as the special qualities exacted of the former are not demanded of the latter.[96]

Florczak, dec. XIV, n. 9: "Et quidem hic testis, tempore de quo agitur, erat puer annorum undecim, verum eius depositio ratione huius aetatis non est reiicienda, nam licet ut non idonei repelluntur a testimonio ferendo impuberes (C. 1757, §1), attamen hac Codicis lege quae ius vetus refert, nullo modo prohibetur quominus adultus admittatur ad testificandum de iis, quae ipse vidit impuber quidem, sed iam rationis usum nactus, quaeque in illa aetate recte intelligere potuit."—*Decisiones,* XV (1923), 131; one may also consult S. R. Rota, *Nullitas matrimonii,* 21 ian. 1924, *coram R.P.D. Josepho Florczak,* dec. III, n. 6—*Decisiones,* XVI (1924), 23; S. R. Rota, *Nullitas matrimonii,* 27 iul. 1918, *coram R.P.D. Ioanne Prior,* dec. XII, n. 4 —*Decisiones,* X (1918), 104.

92 "Baptismus non solemnis, de quo in can. 759, §I, potest a quovis ministrari, servata debita materia, forma et intentione; quatenus vero fieri potest, adhibeantur duo testes vel saltem unus, quibus baptismi collatio probari possit."—Canon 742, §1.

93 Ayrinhac, *Legislation on the Sacraments,* p. 20.

94 Cf. canon 762, §§1, 2.

95 Canons 765, 766.

96 Waldron, *The Minister of Baptism,* p. 149.

D. *The Testimony of One Witness*

The general principle governing testimonial evidence is that a plurality of witnesses is necessary to establish complete proof of any alleged fact. The deposition of one witness does not afford a full proof unless the said witness is an official qualified to testify to the acts which he executes in virtue of his office.[97] Canonical jurisprudence, however, recognizes certain exceptions to this general norm. That is, in some cases the testimony of one witness is all that the law requires as proof.[98] So also, when there is question of determining the reception of baptism, the testimony of one witness who is above suspicion is sufficient to prove that the sacrament has been conferred, provided that this testimony does not redound to another's prejudice.[99]

The phrases *omni exceptione maior* and *si nemini fiat praeiudicium* constitute important conditions upon the fulfillment of which will depend whether the testimony of one witness will be sufficient evidence. A witness *omni exceptione maior* is one who is absolutely trustworthy, and the credibility of whose testimony may not be excluded on the grounds of unfitness, suspicion or incapacity.[100] The other qualifying expression, *si nemini fiat praeiudicium* safeguards an interested party whose rights might be injured by another's claim concerning the baptism. When a material advantage, for example, the settlement of a disputed legacy would be contingent upon the ability of one party to prove that he had been baptized, one witness would not suffice.[101] Therefore, if the proof of baptism is contested because it will be to the benefit of someone else, if there is no evidence accepted as establishing the fact of baptism, a full testimonial proof is required.[102]

---

[97] Canon 1791, §1.

[98] Examples of this may be found in canons 800; 1159, §1; 239, §1, n. 17.

[99] "Ad collatum baptismum comprobandum, si nemini fiat praeiudicium, satis est unus testis omni exceptione maior, vel ipsius baptizati iusiurandum, si ipse in adulta aetate baptismum receperit."—Canon 779.

[100] Noval, *De Iudiciis*, n. 512; Blat, *Commentarium Textus Codicis Iuris Canonici* (5 vols. in 6, Romae: Ex Typographia Pontificia in Instituto Pii IX, 1920–1927), Lib. III, Pars I, 71; Augustine, *A Commentary on the New Code of Canon Law*, IV, 96; cf. canon 1757.

[101] Augustine, *A Commentary on the New Code of Canon Law*, IV, 96.

[102] Vermeersch-Creusen, *Epitome Iuris Canonici*, II, n. 56.

Similarly when the reception of baptism would constitute the basis for an impediment, and thus, against the will of the other party, make way for the dissolution of a marriage already contracted, some stronger proof would be needed. Muniz gives another example in which the testimony of one witness could not be accepted as proof because of prejudice to another. He states that the right of patronage (*ius patronatus*), which can only be transmitted to baptized persons, could not pass to someone who could only produce one witness to support his baptism. The reason is that the right of patronage constitutes a limitation of the rights of the Church and it is the desire of the law that the right of patronage be extinguished wherever possible.[103] Bouuaert-Simenon cite another case, namely, when from the proof of baptism received there would follow the consequent impossibility of another's making use of the Pauline privilege.[104]

Prejudice, therefore, may be said to arise from the proof of baptism when the established fact of baptism runs counter to the best interests of another, or when it will be to his advantage if there is no available proof that baptism has been received. It does not seem accurate to say that a full proof is required when merely another's right is involved or affected by the claim to baptism. The word *praeiudicium* implies something more, that is, that the proof of baptism will be detrimental to the rights and wishes of another person.[105]

A case brought before the tribunal of the Rota, in the year 1911, illustrates the points treated in the foregoing paragraphs. The decision was based upon principles of law now enunciated in canon 779. A diocesan tribunal had declared a marriage null on the basis of the impediment of spiritual relationship. The plaintiff in the case, who was the woman, had acted as godmother at the solemn baptism of her sister's child. The sister, who later died, was the first wife of the plaintiff's husband. Prior to the

---

103 *Procedimientos Eclesiásticos,* II, n. 204.

104 *Manuale Juris Canonici,* II, n. 56.

105 As used in this canon the word *praeiudicium* seems to be the equivalent of *damnum.* Cf. Köstler, *Wörterbuch zum Codex Iuris Canonici* (München: Kösel-Pustet), s. v. *praeiudicium.*

Code the impediment of spiritual relationship arose between the godparents and the parents of the child baptized. When afterwards the plaintiff married her deceased sister's husband a dispensation from the impediment of affinity was obtained, but the parties were unaware of the other existing diriment impediment of spiritual relationship. It was proved (upon the petition of the woman) that, since no dispensation had been granted, the marriage was invalid. A court of second instance confirmed the sentence of nullity.

The defendant subsequently appealed the case to the Rota, alleging that new evidence had appeared. A doctor who had assisted at the birth of the child, from whose baptism the impediment arose, testified that he had baptized the child privately at birth because he feared the child would die. If the child had been privately baptized, then the impediment could not have arisen from the subsequent solemn ceremony of baptism. The question considered by the Rota, therefore, was whether or not the testimony of the doctor, as the sole witness of the baptism, could sufficiently establish the fact of the private baptism. If this could be shown, then the solemn baptism was at least of doubtful validity, and in consequence the impediment could be regarded as non-existent.

The decision rendered by the Rota recognized the established legal principle that the fact of baptism could be proved by one witness. It refused to admit the testimony of the doctor, however, in view of the fact that he was not an absolutely trustworthy witness (*omni exceptione maior*) and that his testimony was injurious to the right of the plaintiff who had proved her case to the court's satisfaction. The doctor was not considered a suitable witness since there was known to be an enmity between him and the plaintiff's family. Other circumstances also pointed to the unlikelihood of the baptism. The doctor had told no one of the baptism, and none of the members of the family had any recollection that there had been a private baptism prior to the solemn baptism in the church.

Even supposing that the testimony of the doctor could be regarded as free of all suspicion, the decision stated that his testimony was gravely prejudicial to the plaintiff's case, and as a result had to be excluded. The decision, therefore, clearly stressed the fact that one witness will suffice for proving the reception of baptism only in the event that two conditions are simultaneously fulfilled—the testimony must be entirely free of suspicion and at the same time in no way injurious to another's right.[106]

It may be noted that in the above mentioned examples the concern of the interested party is not so much centered upon the actual existence of the other person's baptism as it is upon the existence of the proof of that fact. The detriment to his right does not arise from the fact of baptism itself, but from the proof of that fact, that is, if the reception of baptism is accepted as proved. The sentiment of the interested party may be expressed in this manner, "I hope that person will not succeed in proving that he was baptized." Also the *praeiudicium* is not caused by the mode of proof (e.g., the testimony of one witness), for the same effect obtains no matter what proof is utilized. Consequently it seems accurate to state that the only time the general rule of canon 779 may not be applied is when someone contests the proof of the reception of baptism because it will be advantageous to him if this fact is not established by proof. The clause "*si nemini fiat praeiudicium*" is a limitation which becomes operative when the proof is contested by an interested party.

Other instances may be imagined in which the interest of another party would be directed principally to the very fact of baptism rather than to the proof of this fact. Thus, in the case of two Catholics about to marry, one party will wish his marriage partner to be validly baptized for this is a necessary adjunct to their valid union in marriage. His only concern is that perhaps his partner may not be baptized. He does not oppose any proof that the other party may present. He trusts that sufficient evidence is available, for this promotes a security concerning the other person's baptism. Consequently the clause "*si nemini fiat praeiudicium*" seems to have no application in a case of this type.

---

[106] S. R. Rota, *Nullitas matrimonii,* 25 febr. 1911, *coram R.P.D. Ioseph Mori,* dec. X—*Decisiones,* III (1911), 93–102.

The question here is what evidence may be relied upon to remove reasonable doubt concerning the possibility that the other person is in reality not baptized. The answer seems to be contained in the general norm of canon 779, namely, the testimony of even one witness, provided that he or she is trustworthy, or the sworn assertion of the person himself, if he was baptized after becoming an adult, constitutes sufficient evidence.

In the case described in the foregoing paragraph one may reason in this fashion. If the witness is not telling the truth and the person in question is really not baptized, then obviously grave harm will be done to the other party. The law wishes to prevent this and therefore inserts the qualifying clause "*si nemini fiat praeiudicium.*" Full proof is required in a case of this nature. But such an argument would suppose that the witness is not trustworthy. The harm that might result is contingent upon this fact. The same possibility or hypothesis could be posited no matter how many witnesses testify in favor of the baptism. The legislator states that the testimony of one witness, thoroughly trustworthy, overcomes the force of the opposite supposition.

The witness who testifies to the baptism of another may do so either in the rôle of a simple spectator who observed the ceremony, or in the rôle of one who actually administered the sacrament. In the case of private baptism administered in danger of death by a lay person, the one who baptized may be the only witness to the baptism. In virtue of canon 779 this person may sufficiently prove that the baptism has been administered, as long as this testimony is not contested by another whose right would be involved in the claim made for the reception of the baptism. The only stipulation made in regard to the person of the witness is that he or she be worthy of trust and credence (*omni exceptione maior*). When a private baptism is reported to the pastor he will be the judge of whether or not the person is a trustworthy witness. With the end in view of ascertaining the valid administration of the sacrament, the pastor should inquire how the sacrament was administered. When the pastor believes that both fact and validity have been sufficiently established, he may supply the ceremonies and enter the baptism in his register. Proper mention should be made of the circumstances of the private baptism.[107]

The word of a doctor, of a nurse, or of any lay person who performed the baptism furnishes acceptable proof of the fact of baptism, in the supposition that there is no prejudice to another and no reason to suspect the trustworthiness of the witness. The pastor who is called upon to judge this matter will have little reason to regard the testimony of the witness with suspicion if the baptism is brought to his attention shortly after it took place. At such a time there exists no apparent reason or motive for anyone to act deceitfully, or for anyone to have an interest in contesting the reported fact of baptism. When this form of proof is offered at a considerable time after the baptism has occurred, the pastor should submit the evidence to the Ordinary, who will decide whether the baptism is sufficiently proved.[108]

It seems that the testimony of the minister of the sacrament, even though he was not a cleric, engenders greater certitude than the testimony of one who was not the minister. Benedict XIV (1740–1758) observed that the testimony of one witness in regard to the fact of baptism gained added strength if this witness testified to his own act, that is, if he affirmed that he himself had correctly administered the sacrament of baptism, as long as there was no reason to disbelieve the claim.[109] This rule one should keep in mind when estimating the testimony of witnesses.

Finally it may be noted that the testimony of a mother concerning the baptism of her child does not give full assurance if she was not present when the baptism was conferred. Her testimony may serve to corroborate that of an actual witness of the baptism, but, of itself, cannot constitute complete proof if she was not an ocular witness of the baptism.

E. The Oath of the Baptized Person as a Method of Proof

The final agency of proof of the fact of baptism available under

---

[107] In regard to the question of rebaptizing children privately baptized by nurses or midwives one may consult: Cappello, *De Sacramentis,* I, n. 172; Vermeersch, *Theologia Moralis,* III n. 225, *et passim.*

[108] *Procedimientos Eclesiásticos,* II, n. 204.

[109] *De Synodo Dioecesana,* Lib. VII, cap. 6, n. 4.

canon 779 is the sworn assertion of the person baptized. As with the proof based on the testimony of one witness, so also the oath of the person himself is accepted as proof of his baptism only if two conditions are fulfilled. The first condition is that the sworn claim of having received baptism must not be prejudicial to the right of another. If the baptism is contested on this score by someone else, further proof would be required. The second condition is that the baptism must have been received in adult age.[110]

As regards the sacrament of baptism one is said to be an adult when he or she has attained the use of reason.[111] The factor which determines whether a person is to be treated as an adult in the matter of baptism is his enjoyment of the use of reason, and not necessarily his age. All who actually enjoy the use of reason regardless of their age are baptized as adults.[112]

The use of reason is presumed after the completion of the seventh year of life.[113] Canon 88, §3, however, sets up only a legal presumption or a guiding norm. It does not exclude the possibility of the child's attaining the use of reason either earlier or later than at the age of seven.[114] After the completed seventh year the child is normally presumed to enjoy the use of reason. Earlier than that the child is not presumed to enjoy the use of reason, but it may be demonstrated that he actually does. Once the child has attained the use of reason he may personally request to be baptized, and his request may lawfully be honored as the request of one who knowingly and willingly asks for baptism, even though he may not yet be seven years of age.

From this it follows that the person who was not baptized until after the completion of his seventh year could more readily substantiate the fact of his baptism by an assertory oath, for then the law would presume that he was baptized in adult age. It

---

[110] ". . . si ipse in adulta aetate baptismum receperit"—Canon 779.

[111] "Cum agitur de baptismo: . . . Adulti autem censentur, qui rationis usu fruuntur; . . ."—Canon 745, §2, n. 2.

[112] Ayrinhac, *Legislation on the Sacraments*, p. 22; Augustine, *A Commentary on the New Code of Canon Law*, IV, 47.

[113] Canon 88, §3.

[114] Cappello, *De Sacramentis*, I, n. 153.

could also happen that one receives baptism before the seventh year of life, but nevertheless in the capacity of an adult, inasmuch as at the time he actually enjoys the use of reason. If such a person wishes to establish proof for his reception of baptism by his personal oath then there rests upon him the further burden of showing that even though he was not seven years of age he did enjoy the use of reason. The sworn affirmation of the person baptized cannot be invoked to substantiate a baptism received in infancy.

The oath of the person baptized is at times a useful method of establishing the fact of baptism. Its use may be illustrated by a hypothetical case. Suppose that a convert is baptized at the age of eighteen, and the record of his baptism is lost or destroyed. One year later, during which time he has moved away from the place where he was baptized, he wishes to be admitted to confirmation. If no baptismal certificate can be secured and there is no one to testify to his baptism, the only available proof of his baptism will be his own sworn affirmation. This would constitute sufficient proof to enable the person to be confirmed, for there is evidently no question of prejudice to another in his desire to receive confirmation.

When the oath of the person who claims to be baptized is the only proof obtainable, another item to be taken into consideration is the time when the assertion is made—that is, was it made *tempore suspecto aut non suspecto*. This may be illustrated by continuing the supposition of the case mentioned above. Let it be assumed that the person in the case contracted a marriage outside the Church. This marriage proved unsuccessful, and a short time later he obtained a civil divorce. After a lapse of some years he returns to the Church and desires to marry as a Catholic. In order to obtain a declaration of nullity of his earlier marriage, he will have to prove that he was bound by the Catholic form of marriage. This could be shown by his proving that he had been baptized, and consequently was held to observe the Catholic form of marriage. The only available proof of baptism is his oath, taken at the time he was confirmed, and registered in the confirmation record. It appears that this would be an acceptable proof of his baptism and, by consequence, of his subsequent obligation to marry in the Catholic form of marriage, for the affirmation of baptism was made *tempore non suspecto,* that is, on the occasion of confirmation when there was no reason to disbelieve his claim.

F. The Presumption of Baptism

It has been seen that in the law prior to the Code there were occasions when it was licit to presume that baptism had been received. None of these presumptions of baptism are expressly stated in the Code. From this one may conclude that by law no one is presumed to be baptized, and that the fact of baptism must, therefore, always be established by proof. These presumptions of law in regard to baptism, while they no longer exist as *praesumptiones iuris,* may still be utilized as *praesumptiones hominis.* A presumption of the fact of baptism which is still a part of canonical practice is that which is entertained in favor of the baptism of a child of good Catholic parents. A child born of and reared by practical Catholic parents is presumed to have been baptized.[115] Consequently, if the baptismal record of such a person cannot be located, as Wanenmacher remarks, it is more logical to suppose that the pastor neglected to register the baptism than to imagine that the parents were unmindful of a duty so widely observed by Catholics.[116] In this case the active Catholic practice of the parents supplies the lack of juridical proof.

The Holy Office in the year 1883 confirmed the lawfulness of this presumption.[117] De Smet states that when this presumption is verified it would not be allowable to rebaptize, unless the force of this presumption were counteracted by concomitant adverse factors, such as the disturbed conditions attendant upon the waging of a war at the time of the child's birth and during the years of its infancy, or the straitened situation occasioned by a

---

[115] Cappello, *De Sacramentis,* I, n. 190; Sipos, *Enchiridion Iuris Canonici,* p. 448; cf. c. 3, X, *de presbytero non baptizato,* III, 43.

[116] *Canonical Evidence in Marriage Cases,* p. 325.

[117] S. C. S. Off. (Savannah), 1 aug. 1883—*Fontes,* n. 1083.

widespread attitude of hostility against Catholic belief and practice.[118]

ARTICLE 3. SPECIAL CASES

A. The Proof of One's Baptism as Required for Marriage

Prior to the celebration of marriage and as an important adjunct to the pre-nuptial investigation, the pastor shall ask both parties to present their baptismal certificates, unless one or both were baptized in his parish.[119] If the baptism was conferred in his own parish, the pastor need only consult the parochial register for verifying the baptism.[120]

If the marriage is to be celebrated with a dispensation from the impediment of disparity of cult, of course only the Catholic party shall have to produce a certificate of baptism.[121] But if only the impediment of mixed religion is present, the baptized non-Catholic should be asked to furnish a baptismal certificate if possible. The sole exception made by the canon is in regard to a marriage in which there is an impediment of disparity of cult. Consequently the pastor is not excused from the duty of asking a baptized non-Catholic for a testimony of his baptism.[122] Certainly there can be no justification for habitually neglecting to do so.[123]

The purpose of the baptismal certificate in this instance is twofold. It is of prime importance in establishing the freedom of

---

[118] *Tractatus Dogmatico-Moralis De Sacramentis,* n. 301.

[119] Canon 1021, §1.

[120] In the law before the promulgation of the Code the baptismal certificate had to be issued even though the parties to the marriage had been baptized in the parish where the marriage was to take place. The reason for this was that the Ordinary could not grant permission for the publication of the banns until after he had received the certificates of baptism. Cf. Cappello, *De Sacramentis,* III, n. 148; Gasparri, *Tractatus Canonicus de Matrimonio,* I, n. 144.

[121] Canon 1021, §1.

[122] Chelodi, *Ius Matrimoniale Iuxta Codicem Iuris Canonici* (3. ed., Tridenti: Libr. Edit. Tridentum, 1921), n. 21.

[123] Payen, *De Matrimonio in Missionibus et Potissimum in Sinis Tractatus Practicus et Casus* (2. ed. 3 vols., Zi-ka-wei: In typographia T'ou-se-we, 1935–1936), I, nn. 418, 462. (This work will be cited as *De Matrimonio.*)

Catholic parties to marry, that is, that there is no impediment preventing their union in marriage. An examination of the baptismal certificate will make known whether the person baptized has been confirmed, has been previously married, has received the order of subdiaconate or was admitted to solemn religious profession.[124] Also a declaration of the nullity of an earlier marriage will be noted on such a certificate.[125] The items mentioned will be found in the baptismal register. Any of these further entries which appear should be included when a transcript of the baptismal record is issued.[126] In order that the certificate of baptism may contain these latest annotations, it must be of recent issue when presented to the pastor, and drawn up precisely for the purpose of marriage.[127] It is with this same end in view that the pastor is required to demand a certificate even though he knew from his own personal knowledge that the person had been baptized.[128]

The other reason for the presentation of the certificate is to prove that the persons were baptized and thereby to prevent their contracting a marriage with an impediment of disparity of cult or of mixed religion. Since valid baptism is essentially necessary for the reception of the other sacraments, doubt both as to the fact and as to the validity of baptism should be eliminated before the celebration of the marriage. Before the marriage is entered into, it must be clear that nothing stands in the way of its valid and licit celebration.[129]

The fact of the reception of baptism must be proved. The type of proof exacted is the testimony of a public document. Woywod questions the meaning of the phrase "*testimonium baptismi*" in canon 1021, §1. He believes that it does not necessarily mean an authentic certificate of baptism copied from the baptismal register.

[124] Canon 470, §2.

[125] Canon 1988.

[126] Canon 470, §2.

[127] De Smet, *De Sponsalibus et Matrimonio*, n. 678; Davis, *Moral and Pastoral Theology*, IV, 93; Cappello, *De Sacramentis*, III, n. 149.

[128] Davis, *Moral and Pastoral Theology*, IV, 92; Payen, *De Matrimonio*, I, n. 419.

[129] Canon 1019, §1.

Hence he extends the meaning of this phrase so as to include other reliable forms of proof, such as is afforded by witnesses, etc.[130] This view is also adopted by Donovan.[131] The more common opinion, however, interprets the phrase to mean an authentic baptismal certificate in opposition to any other form of proof.[132]

The 1941 Instruction of the Congregation of the Sacraments leaves no room for speculation on this matter. Its wording clearly denotes that documentary evidence is the intended form of proof.[133] If the authentic testimony of the baptismal certificate can be secured, no other form of proof of the reception of baptism is allowable.[134] The pastor is obliged to see that those who are about to marry will comply with this precept. Cappello[135] and Payen[136] consider this obligation of the pastor to be in itself a grave and serious one, certainly so unless he is otherwise certain of their baptism.

The latest provisions made in this matter have come from the Sacred Congregation of the Sacraments in its Instruction of the year 1941. The principal points which treat of the proof of the reception of baptism required for marriage are these: (1) When the baptismal certificates and other parochial documents have to be sent between pastors of different dioceses, the transmission is

---

130 *A Practical Commentary on the Code of Canon Law* (5. ed., 2 vols., New York: Jos. F. Wagner Inc., 1939), I, n. 993.

131 *The Pastor's Obligation in Pre-nuptial Investigation,* The Catholic University of America Canon Law Studies, n. 115 (Washington, D. C.: The Catholic University of America, 1938), p. 149.

132 Cf. Merkelbach, *Summa Theologiae Moralis* (2. ed., 3 vols., Paris: Desclée, de Brouwer et Soc., 1939), III, n. 837; Cappello, *De Sacramentis,* III, n. 148; Gasparri, *Tractatus Canonicus de Matrimonio,* I, nn. 138, 141, *et passim.*

133 S. C. de Sacramentis, instr., 29 iun. 1941, n. 4, c: ". . . inquirendum est prae primis: (a) de susceptis baptismo et confirmatione, legitimis eorundem documentis comparatis."—*AAS,* XXXIII (1941), 300; Bouscaren, *Canon Law Digest,* II, 256.

134 Cappello, *De Sacramentis,* III, n. 148; Vermeersch-Creusen, *Epitome Iuris Canonici,* II, n. 287.

135 *De Sacramentis,* III, n. 149.

136 *De Matrimonio,* I, n. 417.

to be made through the diocesan Chancery of the sender.[137] (2) The baptismal certificates of the respective contracting parties must be obtained. The baptismal certificate is to be of a recent date, executed not more than six months before the marriage is celebrated; and in it shall be found all the items which are prescribed by canon 470, §2, and article 225 of the Instruction of August 15, 1936, issued by the same Congregation of the Sacraments. Furthermore the pastor is not to give too ready credence to the sworn affirmation of the parties that they are not baptized, unless he knows from other sources that they are not baptized. To guard against possible fraud in this regard, he shall inquire from the pastor of the place of origin whether the baptismal register reveals that this sacrament has been conferred on the parties, in which case he shall obtain a certificate from the same pastor.[138]

The requirement of a testimonial of baptism not more than six months old, the warning to pastors to investigate an asserted non-baptism, and the co-operation of the pastor of the place of origin in this matter are innovations of this Instruction. The Instruction does not state how the certificates are to be obtained. It seems, then, that either the persons may attend to this themselves, or the pastor making the investigation may secure them directly from the pastor of the place of baptism. The precept of a recently issued certificate of baptism cannot be too strictly urged upon baptized non-Catholics. Such a certificate may be unavailable inasmuch as permanent records are not kept. If the parties can present a certificate given to them on the occasion of their baptism, that would then seem sufficient. The testimony of the baptism of non-Catholics is useful only in determining their baptism. From it nothing can be deduced as to their freedom to marry. Even though the certificate is old, it may serve its intended purpose.[139]

There can be no doubt that the pastor is obliged to secure the baptismal certificate and to accept no other proof of the reception

---

[137] S. C. de Sacramentis, instr., 29 iun. 1941, n. 4, a—*AAS*, XXXIII (1941), 299; Bouscaren, *Canon Law Digest*, II, 255.

[138] *Ibidem*, n. 4, c, a—*AAS*, XXXIII (1941), 300; Bouscaren, *op. cit.*, 256.

[139] Cappello, *De Sacramentis*, III, n. 149.

of baptism if the authentic certificate can be procured. Obviously, however, upon certain occasions it will be impossible to prove one's reception of baptism in this manner. Various conditions may make it very difficult or even impossible to secure the normally required documentary evidence. Conditions prevailing at the present prohibit many people from communicating with the country of their birth. The church where one was baptized may be unknown. The records of the church of baptism may have been destroyed or not accurately kept. In circumstances such as these, what can be done to establish the fact of baptism? In other words, can equivalent proofs of baptism be adduced which will justify the pastor's assistance at the marriage without first having secured the accustomed certificates of baptism? It is generally admitted that when the certificate is unobtainable, then recourse may be had to other proofs.[140] Although the pastor may be excused from the task of obtaining the certificates, he is not thereby relieved of the necessity of making sure of the baptisms of the parties before permitting the marriage to be celebrated. Therefore some other method of proof must be utilized in these instances.[141]

It may seem that, in view of the Instruction of 1941, evidence of a supplementary nature would now be excluded and that no other form of proof except documentary evidence could be accepted. The Instruction's failure to mention any other type of proof as well as its insistence on a recent certificate could lead one to think that documentary evidence alone is acceptable. The contrary, nevertheless, seems probable to the writer. Both the Code[142] and the earlier Instruction of the Congregation of the Sacraments on the pre-nuptial investigation[143] explicitly require

---

[140] Chelodi, *Ius Matrimoniale iuxta Codicem Iuris Canonici,* n. 21; Sipos, *Enchiridion Iuris Canonici,* p. 511; Gasparri, *Tractatus Canonicus de Matrimonio,* I, n. 141; Payen, *De Matrimonio,* I, n. 419; Davis, *Moral and Pastoral Theology,* IV, 92; Wernz-Vidal, *Ius Canonicum,* I, n. 118.

[141] Cappello, *De Sacramentis,* III, n. 148.

[142] Canon 1021, §1.

[143] S. C. de Sacramentis, instr., 4 iul. 1921, n. 1—*AAS,* XIII (1921), 348. This Instruction may also be found in Bouscaren, *Canon Law Digest,* I, 497-498.

the certificate of baptism, but the canonists did not interpret that demand to mean that no other proof was acceptable, or that no latitude was allowed to provide for unforeseen contingencies that might arise. The new Instruction justifies no more rigorous interpretation. True, the Instruction does place special emphasis on the production of the baptismal certificate, but this is to be attributed to the value which it has in giving assurance of the free status of the parties rather than of the fact of their baptism. The primary purpose of the entire Instruction is to aid the pastor in detecting any impediment which forms an obstacle to the valid or licit union of the parties.

Although generally bound to accept only authentic certificates of baptism, in certain circumstances the pastor is justified in accepting other reliable forms of proof. This is certainly the case when the parties are unable to secure a baptismal certificate. This may be because the original record has been lost or destroyed, or because the church of baptism is located in a country with which it is not possible to communicate.[144] Payen believes the party to be excused if the certificate can only be obtained with grave inconvenience.[145] Gasparri offers as an excusing reason the lack of time prior to the celebration of the marriage.[146] Ayrinhac-Lydon state that when any grave reason intervenes some other proof will suffice.[147]

In default of an authentic certificate of baptism, the person about to marry will have to prove in some other fashion that he has been baptized. This can usually be conveniently accomplished by means of oral testimony. The person whose baptism must be established as a fact may call upon his godparents, parents or

---

[144] Chelodi, *Ius Matrimoniale iuxta Codicem Iuris Canonici*, n. 21; Gasparri, *Tractatus Canonicus de Matrimonio*, I, n. 141; Cappello, *De Sacramentis*, III, n. 148; Wernz-Vidal, *Ius Canonicum*, V, n. 118; Davis, *Moral and Pastoral Theology*, IV, 92; Petrovits, *The New Church Law on Matrimony* (2. ed., Philadelphia: John Joseph McVey, 1926), n. 95; Noldin-Schmitt, *Summa Theologiae Moralis* (3 vols., Oeniponte-Lipsiae: Rauch, 1940–1941. Vols. I et II, 27. ed., 1941; Vol. III, 26. ed., 1940), III, n. 546.

[145] *De Matrimonio*, I, n. 148.

[146] *Tractatus Canonicus de Matrimonio*, I, n. 141.

[147] *Marriage Legislation in the New Code of Canon Law* (new, revised ed., New York: Benziger Brothers, 1940), p. 30.

relatives, or anyone who may have been present when he was baptized, as witnesses who will testify in favor of his reception of baptism. These witnesses, so long as they are trustworthy, furnish by their testimony sufficient evidence for the fact of baptism.[148]

It seems also that, since this investigation of baptism is not a judicial matter, the witnesses would not necessarily have to affirm their assertions under oath. Canon 779 requires that an individual who testifies to his own baptism be compelled to do so under oath. It does not, however, demand the same of witnesses who testify to the baptism of another. There may be occasions when the investigating priest will find it advantageous to ask the persons who testify to swear that what they have said is true. If the priest should have reason to suspect that a witness is not trustworthy, the demand that his testimony be given under oath may perhaps deter such a witness from testifying falsely. Some record, however, should be made of the testimony. The marriage record may be utilized for this purpose. The marriage register generally contains a space for entering the date and place of the baptism of the respective parties. In the place ordinarily reserved for making this entry, or in any other suitable space in the record, the pastor may make an annotation stating how the baptism was proved and listing the names of the witnesses. Also the entire testimony may be committed to writing, signed by the pastor and witnesses, and this statement may then be appended to the matrimonial record. It is important to conserve some record of the proceedings in the event that the validity of the marriage should ever be impugned.

If it should happen that only one witness of the baptism can be located, may the priest feel justified in thinking that the reception of baptism is thereby sufficiently proved? It has been denied that one witness is enough to establish the fact of baptism for a person about to contract marriage, unless some further substantiating evidence can also be adduced.[149] The opinion is based on

[148] De Smet, *De Sponsalibus et Matrimonio,* n. 678; Gasparri, *Tractatus Canonicus de Matrimonio,* I, n. 141.

[149] "Consilia et Responsa"—*Jus Pontificium* (Romae, 1921–), XVI (1936), 111.

the contention that the fact of baptism in this case concerns not only the individual himself but also his partner in marriage. Should it become known for certain after the marriage has been contracted that this person had never been baptized, then grave detriment would be inflicted upon the one whom he married. According to this opinion, therefore, the rule of canon 779 could not be applied, for the reliance upon the testimony of a single witness would be accompanied with an effect that would be prejudicial to another's rights and result in serious disservice to him. Ayrinhac might be understood as inclining to this view, although perhaps he is not precisely concerned with the case discussed here.[150]

Many canonists and moralists state in clearly defined terms that only one reliable witness is required for establishing the fact of baptism regarding one who is about to contract marriage. They, therefore, do not seem to regard this mode of proof as being in contravention of the rule of canon 779. In favor of the opinion that the testimony of one reliable witness of the baptism is sufficient are Noldin († 1922)-Schmitt,[151] Merkelbach,[152] Chelodi († 1922),[153] Sipos,[154] Gasparri († 1934),[155] Cappello,[156] Davis[157] and Woywod († 1941).[158] Vermeersch († 1936)-Creusen[159] and Payen[160] also seem to favor this view, although they do not express themselves in equally precise terms.

This opinion does not seem to contradict the provisions of canon 779. The accepted testimony of the fact of baptism in this instance does not so jeopardize the rights of another that as a result the needed proof of the conferred baptism may not be sought

[150] *Legislation on the Sacraments,* p. 49.
[151] *Summa Theologiae Moralis,* III, n. 546.
[152] *Summa Theologiae Moralis,* III, n. 837.
[153] *Ius Matrimoniale iuxta Codicem Iuris Canonici,* n. 21.
[154] *Enchiridion Iuris Canonici,* p. 511.
[155] *Tractatus Canonicus de Matrimonio,* I, n. 141.
[156] *De Sacramentis,* III, n. 148.
[157] *Moral and Pastoral Theology,* IV, 92.
[158] *A Practical Commentary on the Code of Canon Law,* I, n. 679.
[159] *Epitome Iuris Canonici,* II, n. 56.
[160] *De Matrimonio,* I, n. 419.

licitly through the testimony of even a single reliable witness. It must be recalled that canon 779 refers to the case in which the proof of the reception of baptism is contested. It would only be contested by someone inasmuch as it would be to his advantage if there is no evidence extant of the person's baptism. In the case of a couple about to marry rather the opposite would obtain. There is no reason why the one party should wish to contest his partner's proof of the reception of baptism. In fact, the presence of such proof facilitates their entrance into marriage. There is no obstacle to the use of this type of proof, therefore, on the score that someone else's right will be injured if the reception of baptism is accepted as proved.

With the matter considered under another aspect, it is to the intimate spiritual interest of the baptized party to have an assured knowledge of whether the other party be or be not a baptized person. If the person whose baptism is substantiated by one witness is in reality not baptized at all, then in the supposition that no dispensation is granted there will eventuate an invalid union. In this case the possible source of detriment arises not from the accepted proof of the reception of baptism but from the objective possible non-existence of baptism in one party to the marriage. The question is then—if only one witness can testify, is there ever need of a dispensation *ad cautelam* (of a *non-Catholic*) or of a conditional rebaptism (of a reputed Catholic party), despite the testimony of the witness that the party in question was baptized.

As long as the witness is a thoroughly reliable one neither of these is required. If his testimony is not fully reliable, then the case is the same as when the testimony of many witnesses leaves the fact of baptism doubtful. The objective possibility that the person in question was never baptized may always be said to remain, no matter how many witnesses are produced to testify in favor of the reception of baptism. The question is, however, how much evidence is needed to allow one to feel that this possibility has been sufficiently obviated. According to canon 779 one reliable witness will generally overcome the force of this hypothesis. There seems to be a strong foundation, therefore, to support the more common belief that with a view to marriage the reception of baptism may be proved by a single witness.

Sometimes it is not possible to locate even one eyewitness to the baptism. If the person has been baptized as an adult, canon 779 permits him to attest his own baptism under oath. This method of proof could be used in the case of a convert, who received baptism after coming to the use of reason and who could, therefore, remember the occasion of his baptism. If this method of proof is precluded inasmuch as the baptism was conferred in infancy, the only other agency of proof remaining is that of a justified presumption of the fact of baptism.

If the person can present a certificate of confirmation or of First Holy Communion, then it seems that the pastor can presume that the person was baptized and in consequence can allow the marriage to be celebrated.[161] So also, when the person was born of Catholic parents who were faithful to their religious duties and who educated their child as a Catholic from infancy, the marriage should not be impeded because of the lack of direct evidence of the baptism. If the pastor himself is not familiar enough with the person's background to make the judgment, he may obtain this knowledge from other priests or friends of the family. The person in question may also testify to the religious practices of his parents.[162] When only indirect evidence of the baptism can be obtained and presumptions are needed, the pastor, rather than decide the question himself, should present the case to the Ordinary for solution.[163]

If after a diligent investigation of the fact of baptism according to the principles outlined above the baptism is still doubtful, the person should be baptized conditionally. When the person whose baptism is doubtful is a convert or a Catholic, this is the

---

[161] Cappello, *De Sacramentis,* III, n. 148; Ayrinhac-Lydon, *Marriage Legislation in the New Code of Canon Law,* p. 30; Davis, *Moral and Pastoral Theology,* IV, 92.

[162] Bouuaert-Simenon, *Manuale Juris Canonici,* II, n. 229; Wanenmacher, *Canonical Evidence in Marriage Cases,* n. 496; Schaaf, "Proof of Baptism or of Dissolution of Marriage"—*AER,* XCIII (1935), 306–307.

[163] Schaaf, *art. cit.,* p. 307; Donovan, *The Pastor's Obligation in Prenuptial Investigation,* p. 153.

only way in which the doubt may be resolved. In this way proper care is taken for the individual's own salvation and for the validity of the sacrament he is about to receive.[164]

If the marriage is about to be contracted when there is danger of death, the sworn affirmation of the parties that they are baptized suffices, provided that no other proof can be had and there are no indications which point to the contrary.[165] Payen advises that it is prudent to have witnesses present when this oath is taken, or else to have it executed in written form so that it may lend itself to proof in the external forum.[166] In these circumstances the oath may be taken even though the asserted baptism was conferred in infancy.[167] If more forceful evidence of the baptism can be secured, it should not be overlooked, for the canon states that the oath is to be taken if no other proofs are available.

When the proposed marriage is between a Catholic and a non-Catholic, after having considered the baptism of the Catholic party, the priest must then inquire about the baptism of the non-Catholic. As was mentioned before, the 1941 Instruction of the Congregation of the Sacraments warns pastors not to accept with over-readiness a non-Catholic's denial of baptism. Consequently, the pastor is to communicate with the pastor of the place of origin in order to find out whether the person's baptism is registered there.[168] The Instruction therefore makes it clear that there should be some investigation made of an asserted non-baptism, and indicates one way in which the pastor may satisfy himself regarding the non-baptism of the non-Catholic party. Witnesses may be summoned for the same purpose. In some cases also the pastor may be aided in making his decision by the presumptions of non-baptism as expressed in the reply of the Holy Office to the bishop of Savannah in the year 1883. Thus, if the

---

[164] Cappello, *De Sacramentis,* III, n. 148; Vermeersch-Creusen, *Epitome Iuris Canonici,* II, n. 345; De Smet, *De Sponsalibus et Matrimonio,* n. 588; Merkelbach, *Summa Theologiae Moralis,* III, n. 837.

[165] Canon 1019, §2.

[166] *De Matrimonio,* I, n. 370.

[167] De Smet, *De Sponsalibus et Matrimonio,* n. 678.

[168] S. C. de Sacramentis, instr., 29 iun. 1941, n. 4, c, a—*AAS,* XXXIII (1941), 300; Bouscaren, *Canon Law Digest,* 257.

parents of the non-Catholic belonged to a sect which entirely rejects baptism or does not admit of infant baptism, or if they belonged to no organized religion, then it may be presumed that their children were never baptized.[169] When the fact of non-baptism is evident, a dispensation from the impediment of disparity of worship will then be petitioned.

If, on the other hand, the non-Catholic claims to have been baptized, he must show proof of this fact. As has been said, this proof should be a certificate of baptism from the particular sect in which he was baptized. A non-Catholic party would be excused from this obligation for the same reasons that a Catholic would. In the absence of a certificate, witnesses, or a witness such as a parent or a relative, could be substituted to certify to the fact of the administration. With the fact of baptism established, the question of its validity will remain to be decided.

It is beyond the scope of this treatise to enter into this complicated problem of the validity of non-Catholic baptisms.[170] An investigation of the validity of many a non-Catholic baptism will not produce complete certitude or remove all doubt. Consequently, when the non-Catholic's baptism is of a doubtful nature either in regard to the very fact of its administration or in regard to its validity, a dispensation from the impediment of disparity of worship *ad cautelam* should be requested in addition to the dispensation from mixed religion.

B. The Proof of the Reception of Baptism as Required for Sacred Orders

Candidates for ordination, both secular and religious who, in the matter of ordination, are governed by the law for seculars, among other documents must secure a certificate of baptism before receiving tonsure.[171] The testimony of baptism should ordinarily be the authentic baptismal document taken from the parish register. The certificate of baptism should accompany the petition

---

[169] S. C. S. Off. (Savannah), 1 aug. 1883, II—*Fontes,* n. 1083.

[170] The reader may profitably consult Waldron, *The Minister of Baptism,* pp. 150–156, for a theoretical discussion on this point.

[171] Canon 993. Further provision is made for other religious in canon 995.

presented to the rector of the seminary in which the candidate asks to be admitted to first tonsure and minor orders.[172]

In the absence of the authentic certificate of baptism other methods of proof may be substituted. The testimony of actual witnesses of the baptism can sufficiently establish the fact of baptism to allow the candidate to be admitted to orders.[173] The testimony of one thoroughly reliable witness, if no others can be found, also seems to furnish sufficient evidence.[174] Likewise the sworn deposition of the candidate himself, if he has been baptized as an adult and can remember the fact, would be an acceptable method of proof.[175]

This case in the opinion of the writer parallels the case of proof of the reception of baptism as it is required for one who is about to marry. Here there is no question of a *praeiudicium* possibly arising for an interested party if proof of the reception of baptism is established. No one contests the proof of the person's baptism in this case. No one will be benefited if there is no evidence available that baptism has been conferred. On the contrary, the established proof of the fact of baptism not only does not jeopardize but actually safeguards the interests of the Catholics who look to the ministration of a cleric concerning whom there must be certainty that he is baptized if his priestly ministry is to be fruitful. The concern of law in this instance must be to determine whether this particular mode of proof may be relied upon when such great harm would result if in reality the cleric were not baptized. Again it is the possibility of actual non-baptism and its consequent effects which must be considered in estimating the evidence for the baptism of one about to receive sacred orders.

In the great majority of cases, no doubt, more forceful evidence will be available, but it seems that there would be no objection to using the testimony of a single witness or the sworn deposition of

---

[172] Cf. S. C. de Sacramentis, instr., 27 dec. 1930, sect. 2, n. 2—*AAS,* XXIII (1931), 120–129. This Instruction may also be found in Bouscaren, *Canon Law Digest,* I, 463–473.

[173] Ayrinhac, *Legislation on the Sacraments,* p. 383.

[174] Davis, *Moral and Pastoral Theology,* IV, 43; Woywod, *A Practical Commentary on the Code of Canon Law,* I, 679.

[175] Davis, *loc. cit.*

the candidate himself, if baptized as an adult, as methods of proof in the absence of stronger evidence. In the sources consulted by the writer there was not found any regulation which prohibited this, or any canonical opinion which clearly stated that such a mode of proof would be unallowable. In view of this, one seems justified in invoking the general norm of canon 779 that one reliable witness or the sworn deposition of the person baptized in adult age may sufficiently establish the fact of baptism. This of course supposes that the witness is trustworthy and that there is no reason to suspect his testimony.

If it seems remarkable that upon such slender evidence of baptism one could be admitted to sacred orders, it may be recalled that the Sacred Congregation for the Propagation of the Faith allowed students to be admitted to ordination when only a presumption favored their baptism. The Congregation decided that conditional rebaptism was not to be administered to candidates who were born of and reared by Catholic parents, even though no documents or witnesses of baptism could be found. Children born of Catholic parents and educated as Catholics were presumed to be baptized.[176]

A final objection to this interpretation of canon 779 may be proposed in the following manner. When the testimony is equally reliable and convincing in either case, why is it that the concern of numerous souls about the possible non-baptism of the person in question makes a lesser demand than the concern of only a single individual about the accepted fact of baptism, which he contests inasmuch as it prejudices his interests?

The fundamental answer to this objection is to be sought in a proper understanding of the purpose of the canon in question. The *praeiudicium* envisioned by the canon is present whenever the acceptance of the testimony of a single witness as proof implies also the established fact of baptism, against which prior claims militate for an individual. Now, canon 779 deals exclusively with the question of what is acceptable as sufficient proof of the existence of such an unfavorable fact. It does not deal with the

---

[176] S. C. de Prop. Fide, instr. (ad Vić. Ap. Cochinchin. Occident.), 30 sept. 1848—*Fontes*, n. 4825.

question of what is requisite as a matter of security for the salvation of others. Consequently until such time as the legislator should declare, by definitive pronouncement, that canon 779 is intended to embrace both of the above described situations, the limited interpretation seems entirely justifiable.

There certainly must be moral certitude that the candidate has been baptized before he can be admitted to sacred orders. If the evidence at hand does not afford this certitude, then all prudent doubt can be solved by means of a conditional administration of baptism.

C. *The Proof of the Reception of Baptism as Required for Admission to a Novitiate*

In every religious institute, all aspirants, before being lawfully admitted to the novitiate, must submit certificates of baptism to their superiors.[177] Again the law demands that the proof of one's baptism be presented in authentic documentary form. When it is possible to obtain this certificate of baptism from the parish where the baptism was conferred, no other form of proof should be allowed.

Canonists are not in absolute agreement upon the time when this certificate must be presented. Vermeersch-Creusen[178] and Schaefer[179] maintain that the certificate is required before the postulancy is begun. Beste[180] and Coronata[181] contend that the law is fulfilled provided that the document is presented before the novitiate is commenced.

In the event of a notable delay in the transmission of the baptismal document, or if difficulty is experienced in finding it, the candidate may be permitted to enter the novitiate, but meanwhile the quest for the certificate of baptism should be continued.[182]

---

[177] Canon 544.

[178] *Epitome Iuris Canonici*, I, n. 643.

[179] *De Religiosis* (Münster, Ex Officina Libraria Aschendorff, 1927), n. 225.

[180] *Introductio in Codicem*, p. 364.

[181] *Institutiones Iuris Canonici*, I, n. 574.

[182] Coronata, *loc. cit.;* Augustine, *A Commentary on the New Code of Canon Law*, III (5. ed., 1938), 217.

It seems quite generally admitted by canonists that, when the requisite documentary evidence cannot be obtained, recourse may be had to the supplementary methods of proof listed in canon 779 as agencies for the obtaining of adequate evidence. The reception of baptism may then be established by one trustworthy witness or by the sworn affirmation of the candidate if the baptism was received in adult age.[183] When the evidence of baptism cannot be secured in documentary form, juridic proof of the sacrament's reception shall be submitted to the local Ordinary, or in a clerical exempt religious group to a major superior.[184] These ecclesiastical superiors are competent to pass judgment on the sufficiency of the evidence presented.

D. *The Proof of the Reception of Baptism as It Affects the Dissolution of a Marriage*

In two instances especially, the acknowledged fact of baptism may be the factor which decides whether a marriage already contracted is to be declared null. This occurs when the validity of a marriage is impugned on the grounds that it was entered into with the impediment of disparity of worship, from which no dispensation was obtained, and when it is contended that the marriage was not contracted according to the Catholic form by persons of whom at least one was held to the observance of the Catholic form.

Cases involving the impediment of disparity of worship are generally decided in accordance with the summary process of canon 1990, unless the baptism of the Catholic party or the non-baptism of the non-Catholic party is doubtful and a formal trial is required to solve the doubt. Lack of form cases are decided in an administrative process, unless some doubt in the matter warrants the need of a formal trial.[185]

If the Catholic party is unable to secure a baptismal certificate

---

[183] Vermeersch-Creusen, *Epitome Iuris Canonici,* I, 643; Schaefer, *De Religiosis,* n. 255, p. 277; De Meester, *Iuris Canonici et Iuris Canonico-Civilis Compendium,* II, n. 994.

[184] Schaefer, *loc. cit.*

[185] Cf. S. C. de Sacramentis, instr., 15 aug. 1936, art. 231—*AAS,* XXVIII (1936), 359; Bouscaren, *Canon Law Digest,* II, 527.

and consequently is dependent upon testimonial evidence for proof that he was baptized, will the testimony of one witness, or the party's own sworn assertion in the event that baptism was received after the attainment of the use of reason, be sufficient for establishing proof of the fact of baptism?

Certain canonists are of the persuasion that when the reception of baptism constitutes the basis of an impediment and thus makes way for the dissolution of a marriage already contracted, a full proof of the fact of baptism is required. They envision this case as an example for which the rule of canon 779 could not be employed to obtain the needed proof. The right of the partner in marriage will be prejudiced if it is proved that the baptism was received and the acceptance of this proof in turn makes possible the dissolution of the marriage.[186]

A distinction seems warranted here. When the non-Catholic party is opposed to the dissolution of the marriage, then certainly his right is prejudiced. If the Catholic party's baptism is accepted as proved with the end in view of having the marriage declared null, then the non-Catholic's contrary claim will suffer grave detriment. If, on the other hand, the non-Catholic does not contest the dissolution of the marriage or perhaps he even joins the Catholic party in petitioning the declaration of nullity, it is difficult to perceive how any prejudice arises from the acceptance of the proof of the Catholic party's baptism. On the contrary, the opposite appears probable—it will be advantageous to the other party and in accordance with his wishes if this fact is established. Bouuaert-Simenon stress this distinction very clearly.[187] De Smet[188] and Marx[189] seem to favor this position inasmuch as they mention the use of canon 779 as an aid in proving the fact of baptism in disparity of worship and lack of form cases.

---

[186] This opinion is expressed by Ayrinhac, *Legislation on the Sacraments*, p. 6, and by Wanenmacher, *Canonical Evidence in Marriage Cases*, p. 167.

[187] *Manuale Juris Canonici*, II, n. 56, not. 3.

[188] *De Sponsalibus et Matrimonio*, n. 587, 2º, not. 4.

[189] *The Declaration of Nullity of Marriages Contracted Outside the Church*, The Catholic University of America Canon Law Studies, n. 182 (Washington, D. C.: The Catholic University of America Press, 1943), p. 80.

This case differs somewhat from the matter of the reception of baptism as a requisite for one about to marry or to receive sacred orders. In this instance the objective existence or non-existence of baptism is of no special concern to the other party. Of great interest to him, however, is the matter of whether this fact is proved or not. If the non-Catholic party wishes to continue the marriage, and hence opposes the declaration of nullity it will be advantageous to him if there is no proof of the Catholic party's baptism, for then it will not be possible for the marriage to be declared invalid. In this supposition, since the non-Catholic's right will be jeopardized, a full legal proof will be required to establish the fact of baptism. If, on the other hand, the non-Catholic also favors the dissolution of the marriage, then his right will not be injured by the fact that there is extant proof of the Catholic party's reception of baptism. Consequently the rule of canon 779 may be invoked, if full legal proof is not obtainable.

The opinion described above is supported by a decision of the Holy Office given in 1922. A child of infidel parents was baptized in danger of death by a Catholic doctor without the knowledge of his parents. The child was educated in infidelity. Toward the close of the year 1918 he married an infidel woman. After a time they separated because of repeated adultery on the part of the woman. He later desired to become converted and marry a Catholic. The local missionary meanwhile learned of the baptism. The case was forwarded to the Congregation for the Propagation of the Faith and these questions were asked:

1. Whether the marriage was valid?

2. If the marriage was valid, could the Pauline privilege be invoked?

The Congregation replied that the case had been examined by the Holy Office, which decided that the marriage was to be declared null because of the impediment of disparity of worship.[190] Wanenmacher remarks that the Holy Office may have implicitly provided for the dissolution of the marriage in virtue of canon 1119,

[190] S. C. de Prop. Fide, 1 apr. 1922—Bouscaren, *Canon Law Digest,* I, 511–512. The Latin text of this response, which was private, is given in the *Archiv für katholisches Kirchenrecht* (Innsbruck, 1857–1861; Mainz, 1862–), CVII (1927), 179–180.

if it was not already invalid.[191] If this was not done, however, the Holy Office accepted the deposition of a single witness as sufficient proof of the fact of baptism.

The judge when pronouncing his verdict must always have moral certitude regarding the matters which the sentence defines.[192] If the testimony of a single witness, or the sworn assertion of the person baptized as an adult, does not produce the requisite moral certitude, either because the testimony of the witness is open to suspicion or because circumstances present in the case reflect a sound likelihood that the person was not baptized, then, in default of more convincing proof of the baptism the marriage could not be declared invalid. It seems likely, however, that these methods of proof could not be rejected solely on the score that to acknowledge their capacity for furnishing evidence would be contrary to the qualifying clause, "*si nemini fiat praeiudicium,*" of canon 779—provided that the other party is not opposed to the dissolution of the marriage.

ARTICLE 4. THE PROOF OF NON-BAPTISM

As a Catholic is at times asked to prove the fact of his baptism, so also a non-Catholic may be required to prove that he has never been baptized. This proof of non-baptism as a rule will be a point at issue when the unbaptized person seeks to perform an act whose supervision or control comes within the ambit of ecclesiastical jurisdiction. The ability to demonstrate that one has never been baptized has an important bearing upon the solution of many marriage cases. Persons who declare that they have never been baptized, therefore, may on certain occasions be faced with the necessity of proving the truth of their assertion. How then should one undertake to prove that he has never been baptized?

The term "non-baptism" in its widest acceptance may be understood to mean either of two things. It may signify a negation of the very fact of the administration of baptism, as when a person would say, "I have never been baptized." Again, it may mean a denial of the validity of a baptism which has been conferred. A

---

[191] *Op. cit.*, p. 167.

[192] Canon 1869.

mere ceremony resembling baptism is certainly not the sacrament of baptism, unless all those elements which are required for the valid administration of baptism are present. Therefore, if the baptismal ceremony was invalidly performed, or if it was never intended to be the sacrament of baptism, the one who submitted to the ceremony is still unbaptized. Consequently the fact of non-baptism may be established in either of two ways, namely by demonstrating that one has never been baptized in any sect or by demonstrating the invalidity of the baptism conferred. For the purpose of the present discussion there is meant by the term "non-baptism" a denial of the fact of baptism. An attempt to prove non-baptism will be, therefore, an endeavor to show that the person was never baptized in any sect or has never submitted to any rite or ceremony known as baptism.

In proving the fact of non-baptism, one must furnish proof for his statement which denies the factual reception of baptism, that is, one must demonstrate that an event did not take place. The assertion that a person was never baptized is an unrestricted negation. The denial is in no way qualified as to time, place or circumstance. Unrestricted negations are by their nature devoid of causes, effects and qualities from which direct proof can be drawn. Consequently of an unrestricted negation there can be no direct proof.[193] The fact of non-baptism cannot be directly demonstrated by documents or witnesses attesting that the person was never baptized. A strict testimonial proof of non-baptism would require that the witness be able to testify that at no time had the person in question ever been baptized. It would be impossible for any witness to attest this fact with full certitude, for in order to do so he would have to be able to account for every moment of the person's life.

To state that the fact of non-baptism cannot be directly proved is not to say that this fact is absolutely incapable of proof, for even an unrestricted negation may be indirectly proved.[194] The

[193] Cf. c. 23, X, *de electione,* I, 6; c. 11, X, *de probationibus,* II, 19.

[194] Wernz-Vidal, *Ius Canonicum,* VI, n. 436, not. 22; Sipos, *Enchiridion Iuris Canonici,* p. 884, not. 4; Wanenmacher, *Canonical Evidence in Marriage Cases,* p. 103.

indirect proof is sometimes referred to as the "*probatio coarctata.*"[195] It is essentially a presumption, that is, certain facts are posited and from them a legitimate conjecture is drawn. This the legislator accepts as a proof.[196] Cappello states that the proof of the negative fact of non-baptism will quite generally depend upon such a presumption.[197] The Code does not expressly state how an unrestricted negation is to be proved. It gives no norm which determines what evidence will be required to establish such a negative fact. Therefore it will rest with the individual judge to decide whether the evidence presented is sufficiently cogent.

How then may one undertake the task of proving that he was never baptized? The proof of non-baptism may be essayed in this manner. First of all witnesses should be sought who can testify that to their knowledge and for the period of time during which they were acquainted with the person they neither witnessed nor heard of his having been baptized. In order that such testimony may serve to prove that the person was not baptized, it must come from witnesses who are or were intimately connected with the person and who would in all likelihood have learned of his baptism if it had ever taken place. The most fitting witnesses, therefore, would be parents, brothers and sisters or other close relatives of the person concerned, husband or wife, intimate friends and those with whom the person has lived. If the person in question left his home or lived in several places during his life, then, if possible, other witnesses should be secured who can attest his non-baptism during these intervals. For example, parents could testify to his lack of baptism during infancy and for the time that he lived at home. If the person later married and took up residence elsewhere his wife could testify that he had not been baptized since the time of their marriage. Although such testimonial evidence does not absolutely exclude the possibility of the person's having been secretly baptized at some time, it does nevertheless make such a possibility appear quite unlikely. To be accurate

---

[195] Cf. Wernz-Vidal, *op. cit.*, n. 436.

[196] Vermeersch-Creusen, *Epitome Iuris Canonici,* III, n. 163.

[197] *De Sacramentis,* III, n. 420.

this proof should cover the span of the person's life, and hence should not leave unaccounted for any reasonably long interval during which the person could have been baptized apart from the knowledge of the witnesses.

The assertion of non-baptism will be strongly supported if the evidence shows that the person's family background in regard to the question of religion was such as would lead one to believe that he has never been baptized. In this connection the presumptions of non-baptism as accepted and approved by the Holy Office in a reply addressed to the Bishop of Savannah can be utilized. The Holy Office declared that it could be legitimately presumed that a person had not been baptized in the following instances:

(1) If the person was born of and reared by parents who belonged to a sect which rejects baptism;[198]

(2) if the parents belonged to a sect which does not admit of infant baptism or in which baptism is conferred only upon adults;[199]

(3) if the parents pertained to no particular sect, even though they professed their belief in a Supreme Being.[200] These conditions will be normally incompatible with the probability of baptism. Wherefore, when witnesses can be produced to testify that such a lack of religious practice existed in the person's family, it may be reasonably concluded that in all likelihood the person never received baptism.

In addition to the foregoing testimony, the one who claims that he has not been baptized should affirm by oath that he has not submitted to any ceremony of baptism since attaining the use of reason.[201] To this he can testify, but his oath of non-baptism would not preclude the possibility of his having been baptized in infancy. Canon 779 does not allow the recipient to testify to a baptism received by him in infancy. In view of this it cannot be considered allowable or juridically feasible for anyone to affirm

---

[198] S. C. S. Off. (Savannah), 1 aug. 1883, II, n. 1—*Fontes*, n. 1083.

[199] *Ibid.*, II, n. 2.

[200] *Ibid.*, II, n. 3.

[201] Wanenmacher, *Canonical Evidence in Marriage Cases*, p. 103.

that he had not been baptized before he became of adult age.[202] The sworn assertion of the person in question, therefore, is of itself not a convincing proof of non-baptism. At best such an assertion would only help to prove that the person did not receive baptism as an adult, but would in no way eliminate the possibility that he did receive baptism in his infancy.

Lastly, when a claim of non-baptism is made, an investigation should be undertaken to insure that there is no record of the person's baptism extant in the registers of either Catholic or Protestant churches in the locality where he was born and in the places in which he lived. This investigation supplements the evidence introduced in support of the alleged non-baptism. Doheny declares that not infrequently cases of collusion occur wherein relatives cooperate in falsely swearing to non-baptism.[203] It may also happen that one would have been misinformed by his parents about the question of his baptism. The investigation of records is a measure of precaution against the occurrence of both of these possible eventualities.

This examination of baptismal records should be as extensive as circumstances will permit. It should be made in regard to the place of birth and the various places of residence. In case a person was born in or lived in a large city the investigation should at least be conducted in the churches of the immediate vicinity wherein the person then had residence. If the person has lived in many places or in various districts of large cities, more difficulty will be encountered in conducting the investigation. Even in this event, however, the search should be as thorough as possible.[204]

The most complete proof of non-baptism would consist of these elements of proof, namely, testimonial evidence that the person has not been baptized and that his family's religious convictions.

---

[202] The terms "infancy" and "adult age" are employed here in the meaning attributed to them by canon 745, §2, nn. 1, 2. In relation to the reception of baptism the attainment of the use of reason marks off adulthood from infancy.

[203] *Canonical Procedure in Matrimonial Cases* (Milwaukee: The Bruce Publishing Company, 1938), p. 447.

[204] Doheny, *loc. cit.*

were not of such a nature as to render it probable that he would have been baptized, the oath of the person concerned that he has no recollection of having been baptized, and an investigation of Church records in places where he might have been baptized. Since the Code does not define what is required to prove a negative fact, it would not seem necessary that all these elements be present in every proof of non-baptism. The one empowered to judge the matter will also be competent to estimate whether the evidence which has been presented sufficiently proves the alleged non-baptism, even though not all of these elements may have lent themselves to being utilized. The investigation should be pursued until it can be said that all prudent doubt of the likelihood of the person's baptism has been obviated.

CHAPTER V

Confirmation

ARTICLE 1. DOCUMENTARY EVIDENCE

A. The Confirmation Register

THE legislation of the Code concerning the recording and the furnishing of proof of the reception of confirmation is merely a repetition in part of the law upon these same matters in regard to baptism. Consequently much of what has already been said about these matters in relation to baptism is also applicable to confirmation.

The primary source of documentary evidence for the reception of confirmation is to be found in the parochial record of confirmation. This register, containing the names of all persons confirmed in the parish, is the second of the records which every pastor must keep and carefully annotate.[1]

B. The Registration of Confirmation

The law demands that the confirmation be recorded in two registers—in the confirmation register and also in the baptismal register. In the special book for recording the names of the ones confirmed, a full description of the confirmation is to be entered. The pastor shall record therein the name of the minister of the sacrament, the names of the ones confirmed, together with the names of their parents and sponsors, and the day and place of the ceremony.[2] In addition to this he should make a note of the confirmation in the baptismal register.[3]

In order to satisfy the latter precept it would be sufficient simply to make mention of the date and place of the confirmation ceremony and of the name of the minister of the sacrament. Baptismal registers generally leave a space reserved for the making of

[1] Canon 470, §1.

[2] Canon 798.

[3] Canons 470, §2; 798.

such annotations. If the person was confirmed in a parish other than the one in which he was baptized, then a notice of the confirmation must be sent to the pastor of the parish of baptism for annotation in the baptismal record. Although this is not explicitly stated by the Code, the pastor of the place of baptism must be notified in order that the provisions of canons 470, §2, and 798 may be fulfilled.

The pastor's obligation to keep and to annotate carefully the confirmation record is in and of itself a grave one.[4] Although the sacrament of confirmation is not as important as the sacrament of baptism, nevertheless the person confirmed will have in later life reason to desire an authentic certificate of confirmation. In accordance with what has been said concerning the baptismal register, it also is permissible to entrust the annotation of the confirmation register to the assistant pastor. However, to allow the confirmation record to be taken care of exclusively by sisters or other lay people would be contrary to the spirit of the law, which cautions against allowing the parochial records to fall into the hands of extraneous persons.[5]

If the proper pastor of the person confirmed was not in attendance at the ceremony of confirmation, the minister of the sacrament either personally or through another shall inform the proper pastor as soon as possible of the administration.[6] Confirmation will generally be received in one's own parish, but candidates are not forbidden to go elsewhere to be confirmed.[7] The proper place for the administration of this sacrament is a church; but for a cause which in the opinion of the minister is just and reasonable he may confer this sacrament in any becoming place.[8] The term "church" comprehends both public and semi-public oratories.[9] When the person is confirmed outside of his

[4] Cappello, *De Sacramentis,* I, n. 221.

[5] Canon 470, §4.

[6] Canon 799.

[7] Woywod, *A Practical Commentary on the Code of Canon Law,* I, n. 695.

[8] Canon 791.

[9] Cappello, *De Sacramentis,* I, n. 220; Vermeersch-Creusen, *Epitome Iuris Canonici,* II, n. 68.

own parish therefore, the obligation of notifying the proper pastor devolves upon the officiating bishop, and not upon the pastor of the parish where the confirmation takes place. Of course the bishop may fulfill this obligation through someone else. So also when a cardinal confirms he is obliged to see that a proper registration of the sacrament is made.[10]

If the confirmation is administered in a parish church which is not the proper parish of the one confirmed, in which register shall the confirmation be recorded? The best procedure would be to have the registration made in both the parish of actual administration and in the proper parish of the person confirmed. This answer is based upon the instructions which have been given for the parallel case in regard to baptism. No official regulation, however, has been made on this matter.

If the person is confirmed outside of his proper parish, but his proper parish is not the one in which he was baptized, a further question presents itself. Who is responsible for sending the notice of confirmation to these two parishes? In virtue of canon 799 the minister of the sacrament should notify the domiciliary or proper pastor if he was not present when the sacrament was conferred. This is not the duty of the pastor of the parish where the confirmation took place, unless he was commissioned to do so by the bishop who confirmed. Canon 798, however, implies that the pastor of the parish of confirmation (not the domiciliary pastor) is obliged to notify the pastor of the parish where the person was baptized for the local pastor is the one charged with keeping the register of confirmation and with securing the entry of the confirmation in the baptismal register.

C. *Confirmation Certificates and Copies*

These documents are public attestations of the reception of confirmation. In them a qualified official in authentic form certifies that according to the parochial record the person named has been confirmed. What has already been said of baptismal certificates and copies in regard to their format, requisites for authen-

[10] Canon 239, §1, n. 23.

ticity and in regard to the persons capable of issuing them is also to be applied to confirmation certificates and copies.[11]

D. *The Probative Value Inherent in Public Documents Certifying the Reception of Confirmation*

The parochial register of confirmation and authentic copies or certificates taken from this register pertain to the class of public ecclesiastical documents.[12] As public documents they are presumed genuine [13] and therefore constitute the most secure method of proving the reception of this sacrament.

The proof of the reception of confirmation could also be drawn from another source, namely, from the annotation of this fact made in the baptismal register. In line with its probative value, how is such an entry to be estimated? Since it is beyond the scope of the baptismal record to attest also the reception of confirmation, it seems that strictly this entry in the baptismal record does not afford a full proof of the reception of confirmation. Subsequent annotations made in the baptismal record cannot be said to point to those things concerning the happening of which the baptismal register offers clarification by way of primary intention.[14] Therefore, if possible, the original confirmation record should be sought. However, such an annotation would certainly give rise to a strong presumption of confirmation and would be most useful if the original confirmation record were no longer extant.

ARTICLE 2. MISCELLANEOUS QUESTIONS CONCERNING PROOF OF THE RECEPTION OF CONFIRMATION

A. *Subsidiary Methods of Proof*

If the authentic certificate of confirmation cannot be secured, the proof of this sacrament's reception may be established by the testimony of witnesses or by the sworn affirmation of the person

[11] Cf. pp. 56–59.

[12] Canon 1813, §1, n. 4.

[13] Canon 1814.

[14] Cf. canon 1816.

confirmed. The rule governing testimonial evidence of the fact of confirmation is the same as that which is prescribed in regard to baptism. When another's right is not thereby prejudiced, the reception of confirmation may be proved by the testimony of one trustworthy witness or by the oath of the person himself who received confirmation unless he was confirmed in infancy.[15] The minister of the sacrament, the pastor, the sponsor or anyone else who witnessed the confirmation could supply the desired evidence.

In most instances children are not confirmed until they have attained the use of reason.[16] Therefore, there will be many occasions when the sworn affirmation of the person confirmed, if he can remember the event, will serve as legitimate proof of his reception of confirmation.

B. *Special Cases Wherein the Reception of Confirmation Must Be Proved*

Before they marry, Catholics who have not as yet been confirmed should receive confirmation if they can do so without serious inconvenience.[17] Although this obligation is not grave, Catholics are nevertheless obliged to receive confirmation before their marriage.[18]

The Code does not exact any particular proof of this fact. The Instruction of 1941 issued by the Congregation of the Sacraments, however, requires that the parties present certificates of confirmation to the pastor conducting the prenuptial investigation.[19] Prior to the issuance of this Instruction, commentators did not believe that a document attesting the reception of confirmation was necessary for a Catholic about to marry.[20] In view of this latest regulation Catholics before marrying should furnish docu-

---

15 Canon 800.

16 Cf. canon 788.

17 Canon 1021, §2.

18 Vermeersch-Creusen, *Epitome Iuris Canonici,* II, n. 287; Sipos, *Enchiridion Iuris Canonici,* p. 511.

19 S. C. de Sacramentis, instr., 29 iun. 1941, n. 4, c, a—*AAS,* XXXIII (1941), 300; Bouscaren, *Canon Law Digest,* II, 256.

20 E.g., Cappello, *De Sacramentis,* III, n. 150; De Smet, *De Sponsalibus et Matrimonio,* n. 191; Sipos, *Enchiridion Iuris Canonici,* p. 511.

mentary evidence of their confirmation or, in the absence of this, some other legitimate proof that they have been confirmed.

The Code is explicit in its requirement that a certificate of confirmation be presented by candidates for ordination[21] and by candidates for admission to a novitiate.[22] In both of these cases, if the requisite document cannot be located, the reception of confirmation may be proved in accordance with the provisions of canon 800.[23]

[21] Canon 993.

[22] Canon 544, §1.

[23] Davis, *Moral and Pastoral Theology,* IV, 43; Ayrinhac, *Legislation on the Sacraments,* p. 383; Coronata, *Institutiones Iuris Canonici,* I, n. 574; Vermeersch-Creusen, *Epitome Iuris Canonici,* I, n. 693.

CHAPTER VI

Holy Eucharist and Penance

Article 1. Documentary Evidence

A. The Liber de Statu Animarum

The Code does not directly provide for the availability of any agency of proof from which could be drawn documentary evidence to attest one's reception of the sacraments of the Holy Eucharist and of penance. The law of the Code neither sets any explicit requirement of a parish record of First Holy Communion nor does it demand that a tabulation be made of those who, in compliance with the paschal precept, go to confession and receive Holy Communion during the Easter season. The advisability of having a separate parochial First Communion record as well as of following an orderly method in keeping one have been suggested.[1] The common law, however, does not oblige pastors to maintain a record of this type.

In an indirect manner the Code touches this matter inasmuch as it prescribes the keeping of the *liber de statu animarum*. This register is one of the five parochial records which must be maintained by every pastor.[2] The primary purpose of this record is to enable the pastor to have an accurate knowledge of the spiritual condition of the families of his parish. Among other items which may be noted in this register, there should be an annotation of the fulfillment of the paschal precept by the individual members of the family and also an indication of the children who have made their First Holy Communion.[3]

---

[1] Cf. Schwegler, "A Practical Angle of Confirmation,"—*AER*, XCVII (1937), 174-175.

[2] Canon 470, §1.

[3] Cf. *Rituale Romanum, Pauli V Pontificis Maximi iussu editum aliorumque Pontificum cura recognitum atque auctoritate SSmi. D. N. Pii Papae XI ad normam Codicis Iuris Canonici accomodatum* (ed. juxta typicam, Romae: Desclée et Socii), tit. XII, c. 6, *forma describendi statum animarum.*

B. First Holy Communion

The usual method of proving one's reception of First Holy Communion is by means of a certificate attesting this fact. This document should be signed by the pastor, or the parish assistant, and stamped with the seal of the parish. When drawn up in authentic form this is an official document begetting full proof. If no special First Communion record is kept, the pastor may base his attestation either upon his own recollection of the fact or upon the annotation in the *liber de statu animarum.* In certain parishes there exists a custom of giving the children a certificate of this type on the day when they receive First Communion.

There are occasions when the ability to produce a document of First Holy Communion will be a valuable asset. Such a document not only furnishes proof of the reception of this sacrament but also establishes the presumption of a prior reception of baptism. This document, further, renders certain the fact of a person's Catholic education, for children are not permitted to receive Holy Communion until they have a reasonably ample knowledge of Christian doctrine.[4] Proof of the reception of First Holy Communion, therefore, indicates that one has received at least some training in the elementary truths and principles of Christianity. To be able to prove the fact of one's Catholic education often has an important bearing upon the adjudication of marriage cases, especially in regard to ascertaining whether a person is held in his marriage to contract it according to the Catholic form.[5]

C. The Precept of Annual Confession and Communion

It has been seen that, in the law prior to the promulgation of the present Code, failure to observe the paschal precept rendered the offender liable to serious penalities and that in certain places when one fulfilled his " Easter duty " outside his own parish he was required to give proof of this fact to his proper pastor.[6] The law of the Code is milder in this respect. Annual confession and

---

[4] Canon 854, §3.

[5] This point is discussed in a recent work by Marx, *The Declaration of Nullity of Marriages Contracted Outside the Church,* pp. 82–85.

[6] Cf. pp. 36–37.

Communion are prescribed in canons 859 and 906 respectively, but no penalty is attached to the violation of these precepts. The faithful are urged to make it known to their proper pastor if they satisfy the precept outside their own parish,[7] but they are not required to offer any formal proof of this fact.

The absence of penalty no doubt explains why the Code does not require that a special record of the observance of this precept be kept and also why proof is not exacted. There is, moreover, only a slight obligation to notify one's pastor of the fulfillment of the "Easter duty" in another parish,[8] and Clinton points out that this may be conveniently done when the pastor makes his visitation of the parish.[9] The pastor will then of course make a note of this in the *liber de statu animarum.*

ARTICLE 2. TESTIMONIAL EVIDENCE

The Code gives particular norms which regulate the admission of witnesses to establish one's reception of the sacraments of baptism and confirmation. These norms derogate from the general principles concerning testimonial evidence in that within defined limits they permit the reception of these sacraments to be proved by one witness. No special rules are to be found in the Code which regulate the number of witnesses required to prove the reception of the sacraments of penance and of the Holy Eucharist.

When there is no explicit provision upon a certain matter in the law then a safe method of procedure may be deduced from other laws which legislate upon similar matters, provided that there is no question of the application of penalties.[10]

Invoking canons 779 and 800 as the laws which legislate on similar matters, one seems justified in saying that the reception of these two sacraments may also be proved either by one's own sworn assertion or by the testimony of a single witness, pro-

7 Canon 859, §3.

8 Vermeersch, *Theologia Moralis,* III, n. 372.

9 *The Paschal Precept,* The Catholic University of America Canon Law Studies, n. 73 (Washington, D. C.: The Catholic University of America, 1932), pp. 84–85.

10 Canon 20.

vided that the acceptance of this proof does not jeopardize the rights of another party. The sworn affirmation as a method of proof need not be qualified by the clause *si in adulta aetate sacramentum receperit,* for these sacraments are not administered to children until they have attained the use of reason.

Generally the person's word that he has received these sacraments is all that is required in the line of proof,[11] or at most the testimony of one of the priests of the parish, or of a Catholic parent or of any reliable person. It can be opined, however, that the fulfillment of this simple requirement would not always suffice, for example, in the above mentioned case in which proof of the reception of First Holy Communion is simultaneously to be accepted as equivalent to proof of a Catholic education. If the statement of the pastor cannot be obtained, it seems that this deficiency can be supplied only by the depositions of two or more witnesses. The reason for this assertion is that, if the proof of Catholic education is to prepare the way for the dissolution of a marriage already contracted (on the grounds that one of the parties was bound to contract his marriage according to the Catholic form, but did not do so), then the rights of his partner in marriage are involved and certainly jeopardized if the latter party protests the dissolution of the marriage.

A strict testimonial proof of the fact of the administration and reception of the sacrament of penance, if this should ever be required, would involve establishing the fact of the actual granting of absolution. Since this pertains to the internal sacramental forum and is a matter that will be known only to the confessor and the penitent, strictly taken no other person could testify to this fact. This question is not entirely hypothetical, for an example of the problem occurs in the Code itself in regard to the absolution from censures.

If absolution from a censure is given in the external forum it is effective in both the external and the internal forum; if it is given in the internal forum, the person absolved may, if no scandal is caused thereby, act as if absolved even in his actions of the external forum. The censure, however, may be enforced by the

---

[11] E.g., canon 859, §3.

superiors of the external forum, and the subject must obey until he has also been absolved in the external forum, unless the granting of absolution in the internal forum is proved or at least legitimately presumed in the external forum.[12] If the absolution is given in the act of confession, that is, in the internal sacramental forum, how can this concession of absolution be proved or legitimately presumed in the external forum? The confessor could testify to this provided that he had been given permission to do so by the penitent.[13] So also, if the person was observed going to confession and then later receiving Holy Communion, it would be lawfully presumed that he had been absolved and had received the sacrament of penance.

In a less strict sense, therefore, proof of the reception of this sacrament may be established by a witness who has seen a person go to confession and subsequently receive Holy Communion. The fact that this person receives Holy Communion is in the law equivalent to proof that he has been absolved of his sins, for the law does not presume one to be guilty of wrong-doing.

---

[12] Canon 2251.

[13] Cappello, *De Censuris* (3. ed., Taurinorum Augustae: Marietti, 1933), n. 109.

CHAPTER VII

Holy Orders

Article 1. Documentary Evidence

A. Ordination Records

Under the law of the Code provision is made for authentic documentary evidence of the reception of the sacrament of Holy Orders. This evidence is in the form of an official record of ordination which is conserved in the respective diocesan curias.

At the conclusion of an ordination ceremony a notation of the names of those ordained and of the name of the ordaining minister, together with a recording of the day and place of the ordination, is to be entered in a special book kept in the curia.[1] Therefore in a book maintained for this purpose there is to be conserved an official tabulation of all who are admitted to orders. The canon uses the words "*expleta ordinatione.*" In the terminology of the Code the term *ordinatio,* unless the nature of the matter or the context suggest otherwise, comprehends episcopal consecration, all major and minor orders and also first tonsure.[2] Consequently canon 1010, §1, applies to all these orders. Whenever they are conferred a record is to be made of their administration.

This record of ordinations must be kept in the chancery of the diocese where the ordination is held.[3] The canon directs that the names of all the persons ordained are to be entered in this register of ordinations. This will include, therefore, both those who are ordained for the service of the diocese in which the ordination takes place, as well as ones ordained by the bishop with dimissorial letters from their own proper bishops or from their

[1] Canon 1010, §1.

[2] Cf. canon 950.

[3] ". . . in peculiari libro in Curia loci ordinationis diligenter custodiendo . . ."—Canon 1010, §1.

competent religious superiors.[4] The diocesan chancery must also keep this record regardless of whether the ordination was conferred by the local Ordinary or by another bishop with the consent or at the request of the Ordinary.[5]

Every diocesan chancery is further required to maintain a record of the ordination of candidates for the diocese who are ordained elsewhere with dimissorial letters by a bishop who is not their own proper Ordinary. To this end a certificate of ordination is to be given to those who are ordained, which in turn is to be presented to their proper Ordinary for recording in the archives of their own dioceses.[6]

Does this mean, then, that the diocesan chancery must keep two special books of ordination records—one for recording the ordinations held in the diocese and one for recording the ordinations of candidates for the diocese if they were ordained elsewhere? The wording of canon 1010 seems to suggest this, for it gives no indication that the same record book is referred to in both paragraphs of the canon. Among the commentators Sipos mentions two distinct books,[7] but others suppose that it is the same book which is mentioned in both paragraphs of the canon.[8] Practically there seems to be no objection to employing the same book for the twofold purpose.

When a candidate is ordained outside of his diocese a record of this ordination will be kept in two places, that is, in the chancery of the diocese of ordination as well as in the chancery of his proper diocese. By force of canon 1010, §2, religious organizations whose superiors are entitled to issue dimissorials are also obliged to keep a record of the ordinations of their members.[9]

[4] Sipos, *Enchiridion Iuris Canonici,* p. 484; Woywod, *A Practical Commentary on the Code of Canon Law,* I, n. 973.

[5] Woywod, *loc. cit.;* Augustine, *A Commentary on the New Code of Canon Law,* IV, 459.

[6] Canon 1010, §2.

[7] *Enchiridion Iuris Canonici,* p. 486.

[8] Vermeersch-Creusen, *Epitome Iuris Canonici,* II, n. 272; Ayrinhac, *Legislation on the Sacraments,* p. 397; Blat, *Commentarium Textus Codicis Iuris Canonici,* Lib. III, Pars I, 491.

[9] Woywod, *A Practical Commentary on the Code of Canon Law,* n. 993.

In both of these instances the candidate ordained is required to present his certificate of ordination to his proper Ordinary for the purpose of having the ordination recorded.[10]

Cappello states that the obligation of seeing that the ordination is duly registered is incumbent upon the ordaining bishop or the chancellor.[11] The canon itself does not explicitly designate who is to care for the ordination records. It seems that this office is most properly the function of the chancellor. Since these records are a part of the contents of the diocesan archives,[12] they are under the custody and supervision of the diocesan archivist, who is the chancellor of the diocese.[13] The record should be kept up to date and annotated in a neat and orderly fashion.

B. Notification of the Reception of Subdiaconate

Canon 1011 has reference to the regulation of canon 470, §2, that the ordination to the subdiaconate is to be recorded in the register which contains the baptismal record of the newly ordained subdeacon. The local Ordinary in the case of seculars, or the major superior in the case of religious ordained with the superior's dimissorials, shall send notice of the ordination of each subdeacon to the pastor of the place of his baptism. The pastor shall then record this ordination in the baptismal register.[14]

The local Ordinary meant here is not the Ordinary of the place of ordination, but the candidate's proper local Ordinary, whether he himself ordained or commissioned another bishop to ordain his subject.[15]

---

[10] Canon 1010, §2; Cappello, *De Sacramentis,* II, Pars III, *De Sacra Ordinatione,* n. 576. Henceforth this volume will be cited as *De Sacra Ordinatione.*

[11] *Op. cit.,* n. 575.

[12] Louis, *Diocesan Archives,* The Catholic University of America Canon Law Studies, n. 137 (Washington, D. C.: The Catholic University of America Press, 1941), p. 49.

[13] Canon 372, §1. On this point consult Prince, *The Diocesan Chancellor,* The Catholic University of America Canon Law Studies, n. 167 (Washington, D. C.: The Catholic University of America Press, 1942), p. 63.

[14] Canon 1011.

[15] Cappello, *De Sacra Ordinatione,* n. 575.

The religious superior to which the canon refers is a major superior of exempt religious, for the superiors of other religious institutes may not, without a special Apostolic indult, grant dimissorial letters for ordination.[16] In regard to religious who in matters pertaining to ordination are governed by the law for seculars, this obligation of notifying the pastor of the place of baptism would seem to devolve upon the local Ordinary, namely, the Ordinary in whose territory is located the religious house to which the person ordained belongs.[17] Cappello however places this obligation conjointly upon the local Ordinary and the major religious superior, stating that one or the other is to notify the pastor of the parish where the one ordained was baptized.[18]

This notice is to be transmitted only for the reception of subdiaconate and not for any subsequent orders which the candidate receives. The competent religious superior, however, must send this notice even though, in conformity with canon 576, §2, he may already have notified the pastor of the solemn religious profession of the person now admitted to major orders.[19]

C. The Probative Value Inherent in Documents Certifying the Reception of Holy Orders

The inscription of ordination contained in the curial record is a public ecclesiastical document.[20] Its designation as a public document renders it capable of giving full credence to those facts which are directly and primarily therein affirmed.[21] Authentic copies and certificates drawn from the original record of ordination are endowed with this same value in the line of proof. Documents of curial origin are authenticated by the seal of the curia coupled with the signature of a competent official, such as the Ordinary or a qualified notary.[22] The chancellor is entitled to

---

[16] Canon 964, n. 2.

[17] Blat, *Commentarium Textus Codicis Iuris Canonici,* Lib. III, Pars I, 492.

[18] *De Sacra Ordinatione,* n. 575.

[19] Schaefer, *De Religiosis,* n. 281.

[20] Canon 1813, §1, n. 4.

[21] Canon 1816.

[22] Canon 1813, §1, n. 4.

issue such certificates since he is a notary by reason of his office,[23] and documents of his composition or to which his signature is appended enjoy public trust.[24] Religious ordinaries and notaries appointed by them may also authenticate documents of ordination.[25] The ordination record, therefore, as well as its correctly authenticated copies and certificates always constitute evidence in public documentary form of one's reception of holy orders.

The testimony of ordination which is given to the one ordained is also a legitimate proof of ordination. This document is an authentic certificate of the order received.[26] By this means a public official in a formal manner attests to the reception of orders by the person named in the document. If the document bears the episcopal seal and the signature of the bishop, of the chancellor or of some other notary, it will have complete juridical value as an instrument of proof.[27]

The notice of the reception of subdiaconate posted in the baptismal record is not meant to be utilized as a form of proof of the reception of this order by the person ordained. The Code requires this annotation in order that the existence of the diriment impediment to marriage, contracted by one who receives the subdiaconate, may be certified in his baptismal record. This entry in the baptismal register cannot be said to be of itself a full proof that one has been ordained a subdeacon. It is beyond the scope of the baptismal register directly to certify the truth of this statement. Such an entry, however, would give rise to a strong presumption of veracity. If it should happen that the curial record would be inaccessible, one's claim to orders would certainly be greatly supported by this evidence.

Since this entry testifies directly to the existence of the im-

---

[23] Canon 372, §3.

[24] Canon 373, §1.

[25] "Superiores maiores in religionibus clericalibus exemptis possunt notarios constituere, sed tantum pro negotiis ecclesiasticis suae religionis."—Canon 503.

[26] These letters of ordination are those which were formerly called *litterae formatae.*

[27] Canon 1813, §1, n. 1; Ayrinhac, *Legislation on the Sacraments,* p. 397; Vermeersch-Creusen, *Epitome Iuris Canonici,* III, n. 200.

pediment, and since the impediment can arise only from the valid reception of the order, it seems that by implication at least the entry constitutes an indirect proof of the reception of the order.

ARTICLE 2. SUBSIDIARY METHODS OF PROOF AND QUESTIONS CONCERNING PROOF OF CLERICAL STATUS

A. Subsidiary Methods of Proof

There is no canon in the Code which makes provision for substantiating the reception of holy orders in any way other than by the evidence of documents. Certainly, if the laws which concern the maintenance of ordination records are observed, other methods of proof will hardly ever be needed. To secure the required proof of the reception of orders it would be necessary merely to consult the official documents in the diocesan curia. In the event, however, that these records should be lost or destroyed, could the reception of orders be established by some other means?

Drawing an analogy from canons 779 and 800, Cappello declares that the reception of orders may be proved by the testimony of even one trustworthy witness, provided that this does not jeopardize the rights of another party.[28] The fact of one's admission to a given order could be established by the testimony of any reliable official, e.g., the ordaining bishop, one's proper Ordinary, the vicar general, the chancellor, or the pastor. Even if the only witness were not one of this character it seems that his testimony could afford sufficient assurance of the cleric's identity to permit him the exercise of the functions of his office.

There are occasions, of course, when the provisions of law would require a formal proof of the cleric's status. A minor cleric could not be promoted to higher orders, nor could a priest be permanently associated with a diocese other than his own, unless all the formalities attendant upon such matters had been observed and the cleric's present status guaranteed by a document of ordination or a letter of recommendation from a responsible official.

[28] *De Sacra Ordinatione,* n. 577; cf. Vermeersch-Creusen, *Epitome Iuris Canonici,* III, n. 189.

The Code allows the supplementary oath to be used as a method of proof when a person's civil or religious status cannot be otherwise clearly determined.[29] Canonists therefore mention that it may be invoked to substantiate the fact that one has been ordained to a certain order.[30] Would the person's oath, then, constitute an adequate proof of the orders received? When one is asked to take this oath in matters relating to his personal status he may not refuse to do so.[31] Consequently, it is a useful method of helping to settle the person's doubtful status. If considered alone, however, it would not seem to constitute sufficient proof. This conclusion may be deduced from the limitations which the Code places upon the probative value of the suppletory oath. It is intended only to supply a deficiency of more cogent proof, and can only be given when partial proof has already been advanced.[32] Thus Noval states that even in cases which concern one's personal status the suppletory oath can only be used as a subsidiary proof.[33] In view of this it seems that some other proof would necessarily have to accompany the oath which of itself does not absolutely furnish full proof.

B. The Celebret

The Code provides a special agency of proof for priests who are absent from their home districts, whereby their status in the clergy may be incontestably established. The commendatory letters which served this purpose in past times now assume the form of the celebret. In the current law the celebret is a letter of recommendation in which a competent superior attests the bearer's rank in the hierarchy and his freedom from ecclesiastical censure.[34] It is used by priests who are travelling and who wish to celebrate Mass while on their journey.

---

[29] Canon 1830, §1.

[30] Wernz-Vidal, *Ius Canonicum,* VI, n. 529; Vermeersch-Creusen, *Epitome Iuris Canonici,* III, n. 208; Augustine, *Ecclesiastical Trials,* p. 275; Beste, *Introductio in Codicem,* p. 809, *et passim.*

[31] Canon 1831, §1.

[32] Canon 1829.

[33] *De Iudiciis,* n. 563.

[34] A sample formula of a celebret may be found in Beste, *Introductio in Codicem,* p. 484.

A priest desiring to celebrate Mass in a church to which he is not attached, if he presents an authentic and still valid letter of recommendation from his Ordinary, is to be admitted for the celebration of Mass unless it is known that in the meantime he has done something which would warrant that he be refused admittance. A secular priest obtains this letter from his own Ordinary, a religious priest from his superior and a priest of an Oriental rite from the Congregation for the Oriental Church.[35]

The celebret is authentic when it bears the signature and seal of the Ordinary or religious superior who issues it.[36] The canon leaves it to the Ordinary or religious superior to determine for how long a period the testimonial shall be valid. This of course should be stated in the document. A properly authenticated celebret for the period of time that it is valid enjoys the juridical value of a public ecclesiastical document.

The word "Ordinary" is to be understood according to the definition of this term as given in canon 198. The religious superior from whom a religious priest must obtain his testimonial letter is a major superior or even a local superior. This view is held by Cappello [37] and is defended by Clancy in a recent work.[38]

When a visiting priest, in compliance with the law, presents an authentic letter of recommendation, he is legally entitled to celebrate Mass, provided that since the issuance of the document it is not evident that he has been guilty of an offense which would disbar him. Consequently the Code directs that he be granted admittance ("*admittatur*"), and the pastor or the rector of the church may not rightfully deny this request. This statement is made in regard to an occasional petition. The pastor or rector

---

[35] Canon 804, §1.

[36] Augustine, *A Commentary on the New Code of Canon Law,* IV, 131; Ayrinhac, *Legislation on the Sacraments,* p. 85; Vermeersch-Creusen, *Epitome Iuris Canonici,* II, n. 76.

[37] *De Sacramentis,* I, n. 737.

[38] *The Local Religious Superior,* The Catholic University of America Canon Law Studies, n. 175 (Washington, D. C.: The Catholic University of America Press, 1943), pp. 131–132.

would not be similarly obliged to accept a priest who would wish to celebrate Mass habitually in his church.[39]

If the visiting priest has no celebret, but is known to the rector of the church as a priest of good repute he may be permitted to say Mass. Even though not known by the rector he may be permitted to celebrate Mass once or twice provided that he is dressed in ecclesiastical garb, receives no remuneration under any title from that church for the celebration of the Mass, and enters his name, office and diocese in a book kept in the church for this purpose.[40]

The visitor who presents no letter of recommendation may be admitted when his good standing is known to the rector. The rector has reasonable justification for admitting him if he himself knows the priest to be in good standing or if the priest's status is vouched for by any trustworthy witness. In this case no limit is placed upon the number of times that the priest may be permitted to celebrate Mass. Even though the priest wishing to say Mass lacks a celebret and is not identified, he may still be permitted to say Mass once or twice if the conditions stipulated in canon 804, §2, are fulfilled. From this canon it may be concluded that the priest who offers no letter of recommendation has no right to demand that he be allowed to say Mass. Since the canon merely declares that he may be admitted ("*poterit admitti*"), it follows that he has no just claim to admittance and that permission to say Mass may be denied him by the pastor or rector. So also the pastor is always acting within his rights if he requests a letter of recommendation from a visiting priest. Must he make this request? It seems that an obligation to do so is present in the case of a visiting priest who without being identified asks permission to celebrate Mass. When the priest is known to the rector, the canon does not appear to oblige the rector to demand a letter of recommendation.

The local Ordinary may make particular regulations on this matter provided that these do not conflict with the prescriptions

---

[39] Vermeersch-Creusen, *Epitome Iuris Canonici,* II, n. 96; De Meester, *Juris Canonici et Juris Canonico-Civilis Compendium,* II, n. 829.

[40] Canon 804, §2.

of the Code. The regulations enacted by him must be observed by all, including exempt religious, except when there is a question of permitting religious priests to celebrate Mass in a church of their own institute.[41]

The Ordinary's regulations must not restrict the common law. It is in this sense that Cappello declares that the Ordinary may not make a statute stating that only those priests who present a letter of recommendation may be allowed to say Mass.[42] Such a statute would be in contravention of the faculty which the Code grants, namely, of allowing priests who are travelling to say Mass under certain circumstances without the possession of a celebret.[43] All religious priests, exempt or non-exempt, when desiring to celebrate Mass in churches of their own order or institute, are not held to conform to diocesan law on this matter. But when they ask to celebrate Mass in a church which belongs to secular priests or to an order or congregation other than their own, then they must abide by both the common law and whatever particular norms the Ordinary may have prescribed for the diocese.[44]

C. *Priests of the Oriental Rite*

Priests of the Oriental rite must obtain their letter of recommendation or celebret from the Congregation for the Oriental Church.[45] If the church where a visiting Oriental priest wishes to celebrate Mass is outside the territory of the diocese or patriarchate to which he belongs, his letter of recommendation must be issued by the Congregation for the Oriental Church. This Congregation in a number of decrees has declared that no Oriental priest may be permitted to say Mass outside his own patriarchate unless he presents authentic and unexpired credentials of recommendation from the Congregation.[46]

[41] Canon 804, §3.

[42] *De Sacramentis,* I, n. 737.

[43] Cf. "Consilia et Responsa,"—*Jus Pontificium,* XVI (1936), 112.

[44] Augustine, *A Commentary on the New Code of Canon Law,* IV, 132.

[45] Canon 804, §1.

[46] Cf. S. C. pro Eccles. Orient., decr., "*Qua sollerti,*" 23 dec. 1929, nn. 8, 9, 10, 15—*AAS,* XXII (1930), 99–105; Bouscaren, *Canon Law Digest,* I, 17–24; S. C. pro Eccles. Orient., decr., "*Non raro accidit,*" 2 ian. 1930, nn. 3, 6—*AAS,* XXII (1930), 106–108; Bouscaren, *op. cit.,* I, 24–26; S. C. pro

Thus priests belonging to an Oriental rite who come to America need such a letter of recommendation from the Congregation. This rule obtains even if the church where the priest asks to say Mass is one of his own rite. The documents of the Congregation make no exception in this regard. This is also required regardless of whether the priest intends to reside permanently or is just travelling here for an indefinite length of time.

A special question arises in regard to priests of Oriental rites who settle in America. If after a correct observance of the norms of the Congregation an Oriental priest is granted permission to take up permanent residence in an American diocese, could he henceforth be issued a celebret by the Latin Ordinary? The Oriental priest who is received into an American diocese becomes subject to the jurisdiction of the local Latin Ordinary,[47] and to him he must appeal for permission to leave the diocese.[48] In view of this it seems possible for the local Ordinary to authenticate his celebret. Such a procedure does not appear to violate the rule of canon 804, §1, for its observance would have been duly cared for in the course of negotiations attendant upon the priest's original admittance into the diocese.

Augustine is of the opinion that the two Greek-Ruthenian bishops in the United States are entitled to issue celebrets to the priests subject to them.[49] This view seems justified by the 1929 decree of the Congregation for the Oriental Church which grants these bishops full jurisdiction over the faithful of their

Eccles. Orient., decr., "*Quo facilior,*" 26 sept. 1932, nn. 1, 4, 5, 8—*AAS,* XXIV (1932), 344–346; Bouscaren, *op. cit.,* I, 39–42; S. C. pro Eccles. Orient., decr., "*Sacrae Congregationi,*" 20 iul. 1937—*AAS,* XXIX (1937), 342–343; Bouscaren, *op. cit.,* II, 3–5. It was known to the Congregation that certain persons were coming to America and other countries and falsely claiming to be priests. The regulations contained in these decrees were designed to prevent the recurrence of such abuses. The decree of 1929 outlines the procedure to be followed when a priest comes to America or Australia to reside permanently and to care for the faithful of his rite. The decree of 1930 concerns Oriental priests who come to America or Australia, but not with the intention of remaining permanently.

[47] S. C. pro Eccles. Orient., decr., "*Qua sollerti,*" 23 dec. 1929, n. 11—*Loc. cit.*

[48] *Ibidem,* n. 12.

[49] *A Commentary on the New Code of Canon Law,* IV, 130.

rite in the United States.[50] A Greek-Ruthenian bishop, however, may not give faculties for saying Mass to a priest who in coming from Europe was neither summoned by him nor sent by the Congregation.[51]

No modification was made in this matter by the later decree issued in the year 1940, in which the Congregation confirmed the original decree "*Cum data fuerit*" for a period of ten more years.[52]

D. The Transfer of Priests from Europe to America

It will not be out of place to make brief mention here of the transfer of clerics from Europe to America. The Holy See has taken great care to see that only priests of good standing and excellent character be allowed to come to labor in American dioceses.

The Sacred Consistorial Congregation has issued a decree in reference to priests who wish to emigrate to America and the Philippine Islands from Europe and all Mediterranean countries.[53] This decree regulates the correspondence to take place between the priest's bishop in Europe and the American bishop in whose diocese the cleric will reside. It requires the cleric to have letters of dismissal, to be issued for Italian priests by the Congregation, and for priests from Spain and Portugal by the Apostolic Nuncios of those countries. Priests who depart without proper permission and credentials are not to be granted the exercise of the sacred ministry in America.[54]

This decree applies only to priests of the Latin rite. The transfer of priests belonging to Oriental rites is governed by the norms of the Congregation for the Oriental Church.

---

[50] S. C. pro Eccles. Orient., decr., "*Cum data fuerit*," 1 mart. 1929, cap. I, art. 2—*AAS*, XXI (1929), 152–159; Bouscaren, *op. cit.*, I, 7.

[51] *Ibidem*, cap. II, n. 12.

[52] S. C. pro Eccles. Orient., decr., "*Per decretum*," 23 nov. 1940—*AAS*, *XXXIII* (1941), 27–28; Bouscaren, *op. cit.*, II, 6–7.

[53] S. C. Consist., decr., "*Magni semper*," 30 dec. 1918—*AAS*, XI (1919), 39–43; Bouscaren, *op. cit.*, I, 93–97.

[54] For an extensive commentary on this decree consult McBride, *Incardination and Excardination of Seculars*, The Catholic University of America Canon Law Studies, n. 145 (Washington, D. C.: The Catholic University of America Press, 1941), pp. 540–545.

CHAPTER VIII

Matrimony

Article 1. Documentary Evidence

A. The Marriage Register

The Code in continuation of the practice initiated by the Council of Trent demands that an accurate record be kept of the celebration of marriage. The marriage register is parochial in character, being one of the five record books whose maintenance is incumbent upon the pastor.[1] If this record of contracted marriages is carefully annotated and diligently conserved it fulfills its twofold purpose. The Church possesses definite knowledge of those of her subjects who enter a marital union and the contracting parties have available an authoritative form of evidence attesting their reception of the sacrament of matrimony.

B. The Registration of Marriage

In consequence of the pastor's obligation to maintain a marriage register, there logically follows the further duty of recording therein the marriages which take place in the parish. After the celebration of marriage the pastor, or the priest who takes his place, as soon as possible shall enter in the marriage record the names of the contracting parties and the witnesses, the place and day of the celebration of the marriage, and such other particulars as are prescribed by the ritual books and by the statutes of his Ordinary. The pastor or his substitute shall make the entry even though another priest delegated by himself or by the local Ordinary assists at the marriage.[2]

Canon 1103, §1, determines who shall be responsible for recording the celebration of marriage. This obligation is placed

---

[1] Canon 470, §1.

[2] Canon 1103.

directly upon the pastor or his substitute, that is, upon the one who assumes the rôle of pastor in some stable manner, e.g., during the vacancy of the parish or the absence of the pastor. The pastor moreover must care for the making of this entry in the marriage record even if another priest was delegated by him or the Ordinary to assist at the marriage. The purpose underlying this legislative demand gives foundation to the common canonical opinion that the pastor's obligation to record the marriage is a grave one.[3]

O'Rourke introduces the possibility of assistant pastors having special powers in regard to the registration of marriages. He bases his opinion on the fact that an assistant may receive general delegation to assist at marriages in the parish to which he is assigned. From this he concludes that since the assistant thus acquires a pastoral right *quoad matrimonium,* he also contracts the corresponding duty of recording the marriages at which he assists.[4] While this contention is not unfeasible *a priori,* it is difficult to reconcile it with the text of the canon which places the duty of recording the marriage upon the pastor and at the same time absolves the delegated priest of any obligation in the matter.[5] Even though the assistant be given general delegation, he remains a *sacerdos delegatus.* The canon makes no provision for a transfer of the obligation of recording the marriage to one who assists at the marriage in virtue of his general delegated power. Although rights and duties are ordinarily correlative, the wording of the law prohibits such an illation in this particular matter.

The pastor who is obliged to record the marriage is the "*parochus loci,*" that is, the pastor of the parish in which the marriage is celebrated. Marriage will generally be celebrated in

---

[3] Cappello, *De Sacramentis,* III, n. 718; Vlaming, *Praelectiones Iuris Matrimonii* (3. ed., 2 vols., Bussum in Hollandia, 1919–1921), II, n. 604; Petrovits, *The New Church Law on Matrimony,* n. 514; Chelodi, *Ius Matrimoniale Iuxta Codicem Iuris Canonici,* n. 142; Rossi, *De Matrimonii Celebratione* (Romae: F. Pustet, 1924), n. 103.

[4] *Parish Registers,* p. 69.

[5] ". . . parochus vel qui eius vices gerit . . . describat . . . idque licet alius sacerdos vel a se vel ab Ordinario delegatus matrimonio adstiterit."—Canon 1103, §1.

the parish church, although by exception and with proper permission it may be celebrated elsewhere, e.g., in a church which is not a parish church or in an oratory.[6] In such a case the marriage shall be recorded by the pastor of the parish in the territory of which the church or oratory is located. The assisting priest is charged with the duty of acquainting the pastor with the necessary information.[7]

The canon mentions that the registration is to be made "*quamprimum.*" This implies that ordinarily the registration should be made forthwith upon the celebration of the marriage. Just causes may justify a postponement, but certain authors do not permit an interval of more than three or four days to elapse before the marriage is recorded.[8] However, the obligation to register the marriage immediately is not inherently a grave one. Consequently Cappello believes that even a longer delay does not become seriously sinful, unless in consequence of it the pastor would expose himself to the danger of forgetting the registration entirely.[9]

The manner of making the entry need not be considered in detail here, since this matter has already been extensively treated by O'Rourke.[10] It may be noted, however, that the record should contain the information required by the Code, the Roman Ritual and by the local diocesan law. The importance of a diligent observance of canonical prescriptions in regard to the maintenance of the matrimonial register and the proper recording of marriages has again been emphasized by the Congregation of the Sacraments in its Instruction of the year 1941.[11]

The principal question which canon 1103, §1, raises is whether the obligation of recording the marriage is so personal to the pastor that it is not lawful for him to commit the task to someone

---

[6] Cf. canon 1109.

[7] Noldin-Schmitt, *Summa Theologiae Moralis,* III, 653; Rossi, *loc. cit.*

[8] Vlaming, *Praelectiones Iuris Matrimonii,* II, n. 604, not. 6; Davis, *Moral and Pastoral Theology,* IV, 209.

[9] *De Sacramentis,* III, n. 718.

[10] *Parish Registers,* pp. 70–71.

[11] S. C. de Sacramentis, instr., 29 iun. 1941, n. 11, e and f—*AAS,* XXXIII (1941), 306; Bouscaren, *Canon Law Digest,* II, 263.

else. The practice of permitting the priest who assists at the marriage to make the registration is common. What can be said of this? It appears that the priest who assists at the marriage, whether he be an assistant pastor or merely a delegated priest, has no duty or obligation in regard to recording the marriage. The pastor is responsible for this even when he does not assist at the marriage. It seems, however, that there is nothing which prohibits the pastor from fulfilling this duty by entrusting it to someone else.

Among the authors consulted on this point, the following, while taking cognizance of the practice, do not consider it to be in contravention of the law: Vermeersch-Creusen,[12] Cappello,[13] De Smet,[14] Rossi,[15] Petrovits,[16] Davis [17] and Woywod.[18] Their opinion seems defensible when one considers that the law neither exacts a personal fulfillment of this duty from the pastor nor does it prohibit him from delegating another in his stead. This is not to minimize the pastor's responsibility in this matter, for the obligation of seeing that his commission is carried out still remains with him. Neither does this give the pastor the liberty of choosing anyone he pleases for the task of recording the marriage. In view of the Code's general admonition against allowing the parochial records to come into the possession of extraneous persons, the pastor may not confide this duty to any member of the laity.[19] Vermeersch-Creusen recommend that the pastor countersign the register when he does not record the marriage himself.[20]

When marriage is contracted in the informal manner described in canon 1098, the priest if he happened to be present, or otherwise the witnesses together with the parties to the marriage, are

---

[12] *Epitome Iuris Canonici,* II, n. 409.

[13] *De Sacramentis,* III, n. 718.

[14] *De Sponsalibus et Matrimonio,* n. 700.

[15] *De Matrimonii Celebratione,* n. 103.

[16] *The New Church Law on Matrimony,* n. 515.

[17] *Moral and Pastoral Theology,* IV, 210.

[18] *A Practical Commentary on the Code of Canon Law,* I, n. 1133.

[19] Cf. canon 470, §4.

[20] *Epitome Iuris Canonici,* II, n. 409.

obliged to see that the marriage is recorded in the prescribed registers as soon as possible.[21] The priest alone, or if no priest was present, then the parties together with the witnesses contract the obligation of securing the proper registration of the reception of the sacrament in both the matrimonial and baptismal registers.[22]

To comply with this regulation it will be necessary to bring the marriage to the attention of the pastor by whom it shall be recorded. The canon, however, does not determine which pastor shall record a marriage of this type. Since the canon fails to specify the pastor, certain authors such as Payen [23] and Chelodi [24] maintain that notice of the fact of the marriage may be made either to the local pastor or to the proper pastor of the bride, he being the one who in ordinary circumstances would have assisted at the marriage. Others contend that the marriage should be recorded in the register of the parish within the territory of which it was celebrated, and that consequently the local pastor should be acquainted with the fact of the marriage.[25] In view of what has been said in regard to the place of registration the latter opinion seems more logical and Cappello advises that it be adopted in practice.[26]

If those who are directly obliged have not already attended to the matter, the local pastor, after having recorded the marriage, may send a notice of the marriage to the pastors of the parishes where the parties were baptized.

The Code retains a private registration of secret marriages (*matrimonia conscientiae*). Such marriages are not recorded in the parochial register, but are referred to the episcopal chancery for registration in a special book kept for this purpose.[27]

---

[21] Canon 1103, §3.

[22] De Smet, *De Sponsalibus et Matrimonio*, n. 701; Chelodi, *Ius Matrimoniale Iuxta Codicem Iuris Canonici*, n. 142, not. 2.

[23] *De Matrimonio*, II, n. 1922.

[24] *Loc. cit.*

[25] Davis, *Moral and Pastoral Theology*, IV, 210; Rossi, *De Matrimonii Celebratione*, n. 105.

[26] *De Sacramentis*, III, n. 720.

[27] Canon 1107.

C. *Annotation of the Marriage in the Baptismal Register*

In accordance with the prescription of canon 470, §2, the pastor shall make an entry in the parties' respective baptismal records by noting the date and place of their marriage. If one or both were baptized elsewhere he shall send a notice of the marriage, either directly or through the local curia, to the pastors of the parishes where the persons were baptized.[28] Mention of a subsequent marriage contracted by the person baptized should appear on his or her baptismal record. The pastor who assists at the marriage must attend to this either by making the entry himself if the person was baptized in the same parish, or by notifying the pastor of the parish of baptism if the person was baptized in another parish.

The matter contained in the Code in regard to notifying another pastor has been supplemented by two Instructions of the Congregation of the Sacraments. In an Instruction of the year 1921 the Congregation enumerated the items comprising the notice of marriage which the pastor who assists at the marriage shall send to the pastor of the parish where the party was baptized. This notice shall include the full names of the contracting parties and of their parents, the age of the parties, the place and date of the marriage, the full names of the witnesses and finally the pastor's name, together with the parish seal.[29] This notice shall be forwarded through the local chancery office.[30]

The Instruction issued in 1941 has a noteworthy addition in regard to the transmission of the notice of marriage. The pastor of the parish where the party to the marriage was baptized, upon receiving notice of the marriage, shall enter this in the person's baptismal record. He in turn shall inform in writing the pastor of the parish where the marriage was celebrated that the requisite

---

[28] Canon 1103, §3.

[29] S. C. de Sacramentis, instr., 26 iun. 1921, n. 2—*AAS,* XIII (1921), 348. This document is also to be found in Bouscaren, *Canon Law Digest,* I, 497–498.

[30] *Ibidem,* n. 3.

entry was made. The latter pastor shall include mention of this answer in the documents relating to the particular marriage.[31]

The Congregation's insistence, by repeated Instructions, upon the importance of making this annotation of a subsequent marriage in the person's baptismal record, emphasizes the necessity of a careful observance of the regulation.

D. *The Probative Value Inherent in Documents Certifying the Reception of the Sacrament of Matrimony*

The parochial marriage register together with copies and certificates taken from it are classified as public ecclesiastical documents.[32] Documents of this type attest with full credibility the truth of the information which is directly and primarily affirmed therein.[33] The same may be said of the curial register of secret marriages. The evidence drawn from official ecclesiastical records constitutes the most natural and most certain proof of the celebration of marriage.[34] Since this is the most secure proof of one's reception of this sacrament, it is also the preferable one. Consequently when evidence based upon ecclesiastical records is available, no other type of proof should be accepted.[35]

The matrimonial record establishes the fact of marriage, that is, that the persons named, on a given date, in the place mentioned, entered into a matrimonial union. It also proves the canonical celebration of the marriage, namely, that the parties exchanged their consent, at least externally, before a priest and two witnesses, as is required in the Catholic form of marriage. The document, however, is not necessarily a full proof of the validity of the contracted marriage. It may have happened that the marriage was contracted with a latent diriment impediment for which no dispensation was obtained, or that the union was vitiated by the lack of proper interior consent. If the marriage is later attacked

[31] S. C. de Sacramentis, instr., 29 iun. 1941, n. 11, b—*AAS,* XXXIII (1941), 305; Bouscaren, *Canon Law Digest,* II, 262–263.

[32] Canon 1813, §1, n. 4.

[33] Canon 1816.

[34] Payen, *De Matrimonio,* II, n. 1904.

[35] What has been said in regard to the genuineness and credibility of baptismal certificates is also applicable to certificates of marriage. Cf. pp. 60–62.

on this score, the marriage record will only certify the canonical celebration of the marriage.[36]

The notice of marriage posted in one's baptismal record does not reflect a direct and primary content of that record, for the baptismal register is intended principally to certify only the fact of baptism. Wanenmacher observes, however, that the entry gives rise to such a strong presumption of marriage that no other marriage is permitted the party until it becomes certain that the said marriage was dissolved or that the entry was made in error.[37] Conversely, the presumption arising from such an annotation could be used to the advantage of one wishing to establish the existence of a marriage.

A public civil document attesting the fact of marriage is accepted as full proof of a marriage civilly contracted, for the Code considers public civil documents of the same worth in the line of proof as public ecclesiastical documents.[38]

The Code does not grant similar probative value to documents issued by non-Catholic churches. Wernz-Vidal, therefore, state that documents of marriage issued by such sects may serve as extra-judicial confirmation of the fact of marriage, but that in trials this evidence should be supplemented by the testimony of witnesses and of the parties themselves.[39] Since documents emanating from non-Catholic sects are not classified as public documents, it follows that they do not enjoy the presumptions of genuineness and credibility proper to such documents. Consequently, if possible, corroborative evidence should be produced to verify the existence of the marriage affirmed by the document.

ARTICLE 2. SUBSIDIARY METHODS OF PROOF

A. The Testimony of the Qualified Witness

When the matrimonial register has been destroyed or is unavailable, the celebration of marriage may be established through

[36] Willett, *The Probative Value of Documents in Ecclesiastical Trials*, p. 74.

[37] *Canonical Evidence in Marriage Cases*, p. 229.

[38] Cf. canons 1814, 1816.

[39] *Ius Canonicum*, V, n. 385; cf. S. C. de Prop. Fide, instr., a. 1883, n. 33—*Fontes*, n. 4901.

the aid of other agencies of proof. The entrance of a couple into a marital union is a fact and therefore may be demonstrated by any method which may be lawfully used to establish a given fact.

If the celebration of a marriage depends upon testimonial evidence for its proof, the testimony of the authorized witness of the marriage will always be of great value. The authorized witness is entitled by law to testify to those acts which he performs or witnesses in fulfillment of the duties of his office, and his testimony is equivalent in value to that of two witnesses.[40] When the pastor, as the authorized witness of the sacrament of matrimony, testifies that the marriage has taken place, his deposition constitutes a full proof of the celebration of the marriage.[41] The pastor is most frequently designated as the "*testis qualificatus*" of this sacrament. Within the ambit of this term, however, are also included the local Ordinary, if he performed the ceremony, and the priest who assisted at the marriage by right of lawful delegation.[42]

The pastor is qualified to testify as an authorized witness in relation to matters which he observes while acting in his official capacity. Thus the pastor testifies as an authorized witness concerning the external expression of consent manifested by the parties,[43] his concession of the requisite delegation to another to assist at the marriage,[44] and other matters which directly pertain to the exercise of his office. The pastor does not testify as an authorized witness when he was not present at the celebration of the marriage in question,[45] or when he gives his opinion on extraneous matters not directly connected with his office.[46]

---

[40] Canon 1791, §1.

[41] Wernz-Vidal, *Ius Canonicum,* V, n. 580; De Smet, *De Sponsalibus et Matrimonio,* n. 149.

[42] Payen, *De Matrimonio,* II, n. 1762; Sipos, *Enchiridion Iuris Canonici,* p. 628.

[43] S. R. Rota, *Nullitas matrimonii,* 28 maii, 1909, *coram R.P.D. Ioanne Prior,* dec. VI, nn. 2, 3—*Decisiones,* I (1909), 52-53.

[44] S. R. Rota, *Nullitas matrimonii,* 28 iun. 1913, *coram R.P.D. Seraphino Many,* dec. XXVIII, n. 4—*Decisiones,* III (1911), 313.

[45] S. R. Rota, *Nullitas matrimonii,* 23 mart. 1914, *coram R.P.D. Gulielmo Sebastianelli,* dec. XII, n. 9—*Decisiones,* VI (1914), 150.

[46] Cf. Whalen, *The Value of Testimonial Evidence in Matrimonial Pro-*

B. Other Witnesses

The celebration of a marriage may also be established through the testimony of witnesses who were present when the consent was exchanged between the parties.[47] According to Wernz-Vidal [48] and Chelodi [49] the depositions of two concordant witnesses is acceptable as convincing proof even if the parties themselves should deny the fact of their marriage. The said witnesses may be either the persons who acted as the two witnesses required for the canonical celebration of the marriage, or they may be other trustworthy people who were in attendance at the marriage ceremony.[50]

In a recent article, Doheny calls attention to the fact that witnesses to a marriage are not *testes qualificati.* Although the Catholic form of marriage requires their presence, they are not public officials. For this reason, the deposition of one such witness does not constitute a full proof.[51]

C. The Testimony of a Single Witness

In the case of other sacraments, proof of their reception may be established, under certain conditions, by the testimony of a single witness. Is the same to be said in relation to the sacrament of matrimony? None of the modern authors consulted makes mention of such a possibility, nor could any basis for this contention be verified in the pre-Code law. It seems, therefore, that the celebration of a marriage could not be effectively demonstrated in this manner. The concordant depositions of at least two private witnesses seem required for conclusive proof.

---

cedure, The Catholic University of America Canon Law Studies, n. 99 (Washington, D. C.: The Catholic University of America, 1935), p. 255; Doheny, "Procedure in Summary Cases"—*The Jurist* (Washington, D. C.: The Catholic University of America, 1941–), IV (1944), 16.

[47] Cappello, *De Sacramentis,* III, n. 722; De Smet, *De Sponsalibus et Matrimonio,* n. 149.

[48] *Ius Canonicum,* V, n. 580.

[49] *Ius Matrimoniale Iuxta Codicem Iuris Canonici,* n. 128.

[50] Wernz-Vidal, *op. cit.,* V, n. 613.

[51] "Procedure in Summary Cases"—*The Jurist,* IV (1944), 16.

D. *The Assertions of the Parties*

It is possible that, apart from the assertions of the parties to the effect that they were lawfully married, all other evidence of the celebration of the marriage would be unavailable. This contingency would be realized in the following circumstances:

1. If the marriage was duly contracted in the required juridical form, but the records are lost or cannot be readily obtained, or the marriage was never recorded, and the priest or other witnesses cannot be located.
2. If the marriage was contracted in the informal manner permissible under canon 1098, and no record of the marriage was made and the witnesses are now dead.
3. If the marriage was celebrated in the somewhat informal manner of canons 1043 and 1044, and the registration of the marriage has been neglected and the priest is no longer living.
4. If the case was one of a common law marriage.[52]

In default of documentary evidence to support the marriage, and of witnesses who were present when consent was exchanged between the couple, the testimony of the parties themselves becomes the only source of proof for the existence of the marriage. Under these conditions there arises the necessity of determining whether the acknowledgment of the marriage by the parties can be an acceptable proof of its lawful celebration.

The Code states that the principal application of the suppletory oath is that in which it is employed as a method of establishing one's personal status when other means of doing so are lacking.[53] Consequently the suppletory oath may be lawfully employed to prove the existence of a marriage bond to which one is a party.[54]

The most explicit declaration regulating the use of the suppletory oath as a means of proving the celebration of marriage is a pre-Code response of the Congregation of the Sacraments, issued in the year 1911. The reply of the Congregation concerned the

---

[52] Problems which are attendant upon proof of the existence of a common law marriage are discussed by Dillon, *Common Law Marriage,* The Catholic University of America Canon Law Studies, n. 153 (Washington, D. C.: The Catholic University of America Press, 1942), pp. 94–123.

[53] Canon 1830, §1.

[54] Vermeersch-Creusen, *Epitome Iuris Canonici,* III, n. 208.

marriages of persons who came to Europe from far-away regions. The Congregation was asked whether, in the case of such persons, the affirmation of the parties regarding an alleged marriage could constitute a sufficient proof of the existence of their marriage, when no other proof was obtainable. The Congregation replied that formal proofs should first be sought. In the event that after a diligent investigation such proof was not found, the parties should be asked to affirm under oath the fact of their marriage. When they had done this they could be considered as lawfully united in marriage and their children were to be reputed legitimate. This type of proof, however, was not applicable when the law required a full legal proof, namely, in the face of another marriage or of the reception of orders to which the acceptance of the sworn statement would stand as prejudicial in character.[55]

This response is important, for it serves as a practical norm for determining within what limits the sworn assertion of the parties may constitute a legitimate proof of their union in marriage. This method of proof may be used only in extraordinary circumstances, that is, when a thorough investigation has failed to disclose the availability of the usual forms of evidence for the celebration of the marriage. If no more forceful proof can be secured and if the case is not one which demands a full legal proof, the sworn statements of the parties constitute a proof sufficiently cogent to warrant that they be regarded as husband and wife and that their children be considered as legitimate. When these statements attested under oath have been received, the pastor should make an entry of the marriage in the matrimonial register. He, of course, should make mention of the fact that the marriage was not performed in his presence and that the entry was made on the sole acknowledgment of the parties.

When the marriage at issue is one for which the law exacts a full proof, the mere acknowledgment of the parties does not furnish acceptable proof. Full proof of the celebration of marriage is required in two instances—if the prior claims of an extant marriage are set in jeopardy by the acceptance of evidence which furnishes less than conclusive proof, and if the children

---

[55] S. C. de Sacramentis, *Venetiarum,* 6 mart. 1911—*AAS,* III (1911), 103.

born of the marriage whose existence remains to be proved ask to be promoted to orders.

The Congregation stated that the sworn affirmation of the parties is not a substantial proof *"si agatur de praeiudicio alterius matrimonii."* Payen interprets this to have reference to another marriage by which one of the parties is probably held and which would constitute the impediment of *ligamen.*[56] The only manner in which the person now claiming to be lawfully married could be judicially held to another marriage is when there is evidence to prove the celebration of the prior marriage. If the evidence shows the probable impediment of *ligamen,* then the sworn assertion of the parties alleging that they are lawfully married is not sufficient proof to establish the existence of their marriage. In other words, in the juridical order the parties are bound to observe the marriage whose existence is favored by the relatively stronger evidence presented.

A very hypothetical case could occur if the order of the two marriages be reversed, namely, if the marriage which can be proved is contracted after the marriage which is supported by no evidence other than the affirmation of its contracting parties. Suppose that a man contracted a marriage in Europe, but here and now can produce no evidence of that fact. Later he comes to America and, concealing the fact of this prior marriage, succeeds in marrying again before a priest and witnesses. Later his first wife comes to America. In a truly contrite spirit he wishes to discontinue his second marriage and return to her. He is prevented from doing so, however, through lack of evidence to show that he ever contracted such a marriage, though he and his first wife are willing to swear to the existence of the marriage they contracted. According to the response this is not a sufficient proof *"si agatur de praeiudicio alterius matrimonii."*

This condition apparently would also be applicable in relation to the later marriage which in the eyes of the law is supported by stronger evidence. The dual affirmation of the parties could not establish proof of the actual existent impediment of *ligamen,* and in the external forum the latter marriage would be favored by the

[56] *De Matrimonio,* II, n. 1930.

evidence of its celebration. The ability to prove the existence of a marriage is not essential to its validity. If the first marriage was validly contracted in God's sight it remains such even though there is no evidence to prove this fact in the juridical order. It is quite possible, therefore, for a conflict to arise between the internal and external forums. The remedy in the external forum would have to be sought in the feasibility of impugning the validity of the second marriage on some other grounds. Should such a case ever occur, in which, namely, the rules which govern the procedure in the external forum fail to make adequate provision for consulting the fundamental needs of individual consciences, perhaps the best procedure would be to explore the possibility of a solution in the internal forum by enlisting the aid of the Sacred Penitentiary.

The sworn affirmation of the parties does not constitute sufficient proof of their marriage and of the legitimacy of their children in the event that the children born of the marriage should wish to be promoted to holy orders. A dispensation would have to be petitioned or a more extensive proof of the parents' marriage would have to be submitted.

APPENDIX

Extreme Unction

Regulations governing formal proof of the reception of extreme unction are not found in the Code. The reason why the law does not demand that one be able to prove his reception of this sacrament is readily understandable. It is principally necessary that one be capable of proving that he has received a certain sacrament when as a result of this reception definite juridical consequences will follow. These consequences will frequently affect not only the individual himself but also his associations with others. Records must be kept, therefore, of the administration of those sacraments which have a particular social aspect, and the law must determine what evidence shall be required to establish the fact of their reception.

The effects produced by the sacrament of extreme unction are confined to the internal forum and respect the recipient's relationship with God rather than with human individuals. Consequently it is not necessary that there be retained external evidence of the reception of this sacrament insofar as this affects the person's status in the society which is the Church.

The importance of this sacrament to the welfare of the soul is inculcated by the Code when it states that it is not lawful for anyone to neglect extreme unction.[1] Although the Code does not require that proof be offered of the reception of extreme unction or demand that a record of its administration be maintained, there should never be left unsolved any doubt as to whether or not this sacrament has been received by one who is in danger of death.

Should the infirm person during his illness be transferred from one place to another, e.g., from his home to a hospital, and thus come under the care of a different priest, there might possibly arise some doubt as to whether the person had been anointed.

[1] Canon 944.

Since in a case of necessity any priest may administer extreme unction,[2] the priest who confers the sacrament is entitled to attest his administration either verbally or in a written statement. If the person who is ill is unable to inform the priest then the reliable word of a Catholic relative or nurse who had attended the patient and witnessed the anointing would surely suffice.

Should the priest have reason to disbelieve or suspect the word of the witness, then he should endeavor to contact the priest who originally visited the sick person. If the urgency of the case does not permit this and there is no more than some questionable reason to lead the priest to believe that the person may already have been anointed, the difficulty should be solved by means of a conditional administration of the sacrament. In the event that no well-founded doubt is present and that no reason militates for believing that the person was previously anointed, the priest should of course administer extreme unction absolutely.

[2] Canon 938, §2.

CONCLUSIONS

1. THE testimony of even one thoroughly reliable witness or the sworn assertion of the person who was baptized after having attained the use of reason may constitute sufficient proof of the reception of baptism when this is required for marriage, for admission to sacred orders, and for admission to a novitiate.

2. These same methods of proof are adequate when the proof of the reception of baptism has a bearing upon the dissolution of a marriage already contracted, if the other party does not contest the declaration of nullity. If, however, the other party to the marriage opposes its dissolution, a full legal proof of the reception of baptism is required.

3. The oath of the person baptized in adult age is an adequate method of establishing the fact of baptism, especially if the oath was taken *tempore non suspecto*.

4. Moral certitude of the negative fact of non-baptism may be obtained from a proof based upon the testimony of witnesses, the sworn assertion of the person in question and an examination of the baptismal records of the churches in the locality in which the baptism would in all likelihood have been conferred.

5. The norms of canons 779 and 800, by an analogy of law, may be applied with relation to the sacraments of the Holy Eucharist and penance.

6. The testimony of any trustworthy witness furnishes sufficient proof of the reception of orders, at least to permit the cleric to exercise the ordinary functions of his office. The suppletory oath, however, is not of itself a complete proof of the reception of orders.

7. Granted that there is no question of a concurrence of episcopal jurisdiction, it seems likely that the Greek-Ruthenian Bishops in the United States may issue celebrets to the priests subject to their jurisdiction. It also seems probable that other Oriental priests permanently established in dioceses of the United

States may receive their celebrets from the Latin Ordinaries to which they are subject. This of course supposes that all the norms of the Congregation for the Oriental Church have been observed in the negotiations attendant upon the priest's original entrance into the country.

8. The existence of a marriage may not be substantiated by the testimony of one witness alone.

9. In default of other evidence the assertions of the parties may establish the fact of their marriage, if this is not to place an obstacle in the way of another marriage by which one or the other of the parties is probably held and which is supported by more cogent proof. A marriage proved in this manner allows the children to be considered as legitimate unless they should ask to be promoted to sacred orders. In that event a precautionary dispensation would have to be petitioned.

BIBLIOGRAPHY

SOURCES

Acta Apostolicae Sedis, Commentarium Officiale, Romae, 1909–

Acta et Decreta Sacrorum Conciliorum Recentiorum, Collectio Lacensis, 7 vols., Friburgi Brisgoviae, 1870–1890.

Acta Sanctae Sedis, 41 vols., Romae, 1865–1908.

Bullarium Benedicti XIV, 3 vols. in 4, Prati, 1845–1847.

Codex Iuris Canonici Pii X Pontificis Maximi iussu digestus Benedicti XIV auctoritate promulgatus, Romae: Typis Polyglottis Vaticanis, 1936.

Codicis Iuris Canonici Fontes cura Emi. Petri Card. Gasparri Editi, 9 vols., Romae (postea Civitate Vaticana): Typis Polyglottis Vaticanis, 1923–1939 (Vols. VII, VIII et IX ed. *cura et studio Emi. Iustiniani Card. Serédi*).

Collectanea S. Congregationis de Propaganda Fide, 2 vols., Romae: Typographia Polyglotta S. C. de Propaganda Fide, 1907.

Concilii Tridentini Diariorum, Actorum, Epistolarum, Tractatuum Nova Collectio, ed. Societas Goerresiana, 13 vols., Friburgi Brisgoviae: B. Herder, 1901–1938.

Corpus Iuris Canonici, Editio Lipsiensis II post Aemilii Ludovici Richteri curas instruxit Aemilius Friedberg, 2 vols., Lipsiae: Ex Officina Bernhardi Tauchnitz, 1879–1881. Editio anastatice repetita, Lipsiae: Tauchnitz, 1928.

Hinschius, Paulus, *Decretales Pseudo-Isidorianae et Capitula Angilramni,* Lipsiae: Ex Officina Bernhardi Tauchnitz, 1863.

Jaffé, Philippus, *Regesta Pontificum Romanorum ab condita Ecclesia ad annum post Christum natum MCXCVIII,* 2. ed. correctam et auctam auspiciis G. Wattenbach, curaverunt S. Loewenfeld, F. Kaltenbrunner, P. Ewald, 2 vols. in 1, Lipsiae, 1885–1888.

Mansi, J. D., *Sacrorum Conciliorum Nova et Amplissima Collectio,* 53 vols. in 60, Parisiis, 1901–1927.

Pallottini, S., *Collectio Omnium Conclusionum et Resolutionum Quae in causis propositis apud Sacram Congregationem Cardinalium S. Concilii Tridentini interpretum Prodierunt ab eius institutione anno MDLXIV ad MDCCCLX, distinctis titulis alphebetico ordine per materias digesta,* 18 vols., Romae, 1868–1893.

Potthast, Augustus, *Regesta Pontificum Romanorum,* 2 vols., Berolini: R. De Becker, 1874–1875.

Quinque Compilationes Antiquae Nec Non Collectio Canonum Lipsiensis, recognovit et adnotatione critica instruxit Aemilius Friedberg, Lipsiae: Ex Officina Bernhardi Tauchnitz, 1882.

Rituale Romanum, Pauli V Pontificis Maximi iussu editum, Antverpiae, 1614.

Rituale Romanum, Pauli V Pontificis Maximi iussu editum aliorumque Pontificum cura recognitum atque auctoritate Sanctissimi D. N. Pii Papae XI ad normam codicis iuris canonici accomodatum, ed. juxta typicam, Romae: Desclée et Socii, 1935.

S. Romanae Rotae Decisiones Recentiores, 19 parts in 25 vols., Francofurti-Aureliae-Romae, 1623–1703.

S. Romanae Rotae Decisiones seu Sententiae, 24 vols., Romae: Typis Polyglottis Vaticanis, 1912–1940.

Thesaurus Resolutionum Sacrae Congregationis Concilii, 167 vols., Romae, 1718–1908.

AUTHORS

AYRINHAC, H. A., *Legislation on the Sacraments,* New York-London: Longmans, Green and Co., 1928.

AYRINHAC, H. A.,-Lydon, P. J., *Marriage Legislation in the New Code of Canon Law,* new revised edition, New York: Benziger Brothers, 1939.

(Bachofen), Charles Augustine, *A Commentary on the New Code of Canon Law,* 8 vols., St. Louis: B. Herder Book Co., 1925–1938. Vol. I, 6. ed., 1931; Vol. II, 6. ed., 1936; Vol. III, 5. ed., 1938; Vol. IV, 3. ed., 1925; Vol. V, 5. ed., 1935; Vol. VI, 3. ed., 1931; Vol. VII, 3. ed., 1930; Vol. VIII, 3. ed., 1931.

BANGEN, J. H., *Instructio Practica de Sponsalibus et Matrimonio,* 3 titles in 1 vol., Monasterii, 1858–1860.

BENEDICTUS XIV, *De Synodo Dioecesana,* 4 vols., Lovanii, 1763.

BESTE, U., *Introductio in Codicem,* Collegeville, Minnesota: St. John's Abbey Press, 1938.

BLAT, ALBERTUS, *Commentarium Textus Codicis Iuris Canonici,* 5 vols. in 6, Romae: Ex Typographia Pontificia in Instituto Pii IX, 1920–1927.

BOUSCAREN, T. LINCOLN, *Canon Law Digest,* 2 vols., Milwaukee: Bruce Publishing Co., Vol. I, 1934; Vol. II, 1943.

BOUUAERT, F. CLAEYS-SIMENON, G., *Manuale Juris Canonici,* 3 vols., Gandae et Leodii: Apud Auctores, 1930–1931. Vol. I, 3. ed., 1930; Vol. II, 1931, Vol. III, 3. ed., 1931.

CAPPELLO, F., *Tractatus Canonico-Moralis de Sacramentis,* 3 vols. in 6, Taurinorum Augustae: Marietti, 1935–1939. Vol. I, 3. ed., 1938; Vol. II, Pars I, 3. ed., 1938; Vol. II, 1932; Vol. II, Pars III, 1935; Vol. III, Partes I et II, 4. ed., 1939.

———, *De Censuris,* 3. ed., Taurinorum Augustae: Marietti, 1933.

CARRIÈRE, J., *Praelectiones de Matrimonio,* 2 vols., Parisiis, 1837.

CHELODI, *Ius Matrimoniale Iuxta Codicem Iuris Canonici,* 3. ed., Tridenti: Libr. Edit. Tridentum, 1921.

Clancy, P., *The Local Religious Superior,* The Catholic University of America Canon Law Studies, n. 175, Washington, D. C.: The Catholic University of America Press, 1943.

Clinton, Connell, *The Paschal Precept,* The Catholic University of America Canon Law Studies, n. 73, Washington, D. C.: The Catholic University of America Press, 1932.

Coronata, Matthaeus Conte a, *Institutiones Iuris Canonici,* 5 vols., Romae: Marietti, 1933–1939. Vols. I et II, 2. ed., 1939; Vol. III, 1933; Vol. IV, 1935; Vol. V, 1936.

Davis, H., *Moral and Pastoral Theology,* 3. ed., 4 vols., New York: Sheed and Ward, 1938.

De Luca, I. B., *Theatrum Veritatis et Iustitiae,* 16 vols., Coloniae Agrippinæ, 1706.

De Meester, A., *Juris Canonici et Juris Canonico-Civilis Compendium,* nova ed., 3 vols. in 4, Brugis: Desclée, De Brouwer, 1921–1928.

De Smet, A., *Tractatus Dogmatico-Moralis De Sacramentis,* 2. ed., Brugis: Car. Beyaert, 1927.

———, *De Sponsalibus et Matrimonio,* 4. ed., Brugis: Car. Beyaert, 1927.

Devoti, I., *Institutionum Canonicarum Libri IV,* 4. ed. Romana, Leodii, 1874.

Dillon, R., *Common Law Marriage,* The Catholic University of America Canon Law Studies, n. 153, Washington, D. C.: The Catholic University of America Press, 1942.

Doheny, William J., *Canonical Procedure in Matrimonial Cases,* Milwaukee: The Bruce Publishing Co., 1938.

Donovan, J., *The Pastor's Obligation in Pre-nuptial Investigation,* The Catholic University of America Canon Law Studies, n. 115, Washington, D. C.: The Catholic University of America Press, 1938.

Esmein, A., *Le Mariage En Droit Canonique,* 2. ed., 2 vols., Paris: Recueil Sirey, 1929–1935. Vol. I, ed. R. Génestal, 1929; Vol. II, ed. R. Génestal-J. Dauvillier, 1935.

Fagnanus, P., *Ius Canonicum seu Commentaria Absolutissima in Quinque Libros Decretalium,* 5 vols., Venetiis, 1696.

Fanfani, L., *De Iure Parochorum,* 2. ed., Romae: Marietti, 1929.

Farinacius, P., *Tractatus de Testibus,* Venetiis, 1609.

Ferraris, F. L., *Prompta Bibliotheca, Canonica, Iuridica, Moralis, Theologica, necnon Ascetica, Polemica, Rubricistica, Historica,* 9 vols., Romae, 1885–1899.

Gasparri, P., *Tractatus Canonicus de Matrimonio,* 2 vols., Parisiis, 1891–1892.

———, *Tractatus Canonicus de Matrimonio,* ed. nova ad mentem Codicis I. C., 2 vols., Typis Polyglottis Vaticanis, 1932.

———, *Tractatus Canonicus de Sacra Ordinatione,* 2 vols., Parisiis, 1893–1894.

Giraldi, U., *Animadversiones et Additamenta ad Augustinum Barbosam De Officio et Potestate Parochi,* Romae, 1774.

HOSTIENSIS, CARDINALIS (Henricus de Segusia), *Commentaria in Quinque Libros Decretalium,* 3 vols., Venetiis, 1581.

———, *Summa Aurea,* Venetiis, 1570.

KÖSTLER, R., *Wörterbuch zum Codex Iuris Canonici,* München: Kösel-Pustet, 1927–1929.

LEGA, M., *Praelectiones De Iudiciis Ecclesiasticis,* 2 books in 4 vols., Romae, 1896–1901.

LEURENIUS, P., *Forum Ecclesiasticum,* 5 vols., Venetiis, 1729.

LOUIS, WILLIAM, *Diocesan Archives,* The Catholic University of America Canon Law Studies, n. 137, Washington, D. C.: The Catholic University of America Press, 1941.

LUCIDI, A., *De Visitatione Sacrorum Liminum,* 3. ed. (aucta per Iosephum Schneider), 3 vols., Romae, 1883.

MANY, S., *Praelectiones de Missa,* Parisiis, 1903.

MARX, A., *The Declaration of Nullity of Marriages Contracted Outside the Church,* The Catholic University of America Canon Law Studies, n. 182, Washington, D. C.: The Catholic University of America Press, 1943.

MASCARDUS, I., *Conclusiones Omnium Probationum Quae in Utroque Iure Quotidie Versantur,* 3 vols., Venetiis, 1593.

MCDEVITT, G., *Legitimacy and Legitimation,* The Catholic University of America Canon Law Studies, n. 138, Washington, D. C.: The Catholic University of America Press, 1941.

MERKELBACH, B., *Summa Theologiae Moralis,* 3 vols., Parisiis: Desclée, de Brouwer et Soc., 1936–1938. Vols. I et II, 3. ed., 1938; Vol. II, 2. ed., 1936.

MONACELLI, F., *Formularium Legale Practicum Fori Ecclesiastici,* Venetiis, 1706.

MUNIZ, T., *Procedimientos Eclesiásticos,* 2. ed., 3 vols., Sevilla: Lib. de Sobrino de Izquierdo, 1926.

NAVARRUS (de Azpilcueta), M., *Consiliorum seu Responsorum Quinque Libri,* Venetiis, 1621.

NOLDIN, H.–SCHMITT, A., *Summa Theologiae Moralis,* 3 vols., Oeniponte-Lipsiae: Rauch, 1940–1941. Vols. I et II, 27. ed., 1941; Vol. III, 26. ed., 1940.

NOVAL, I., *Commentarium Codicis Iuris Canonici,* Lib. IV, *De Processibus,* 2 vols., Pars I, *De Iudiciis,* Romae: Marietti, 1920.

O'ROURKE, J., *Parish Registers,* The Catholic University of America Canon Law Studies, n. 88, Washington, D. C.: The Catholic University of America, 1934.

PANORMITANUS, ABBAS (Nicholaus de Tudeschis), *Commentaria in Quinque Libros Decretalium,* Venetiis, 1588.

PAYEN, G., *De Matrimonio in Missionibus ac Potissimum in Sinis Tractatus Practicus et Casus,* 2. ed., 3 vols., Zi-ka-wei; In Typographia T'ou-se-we, 1935–1936.

PAX JORDANUS, *Elucubrationes Diversae,* 3 vols., Coloniae Allobrogum et Lugduni, 1729.

PETROVITS, J., *The New Church Law on Matrimony,* 2. ed., Philadelphia: John Joseph McVey, 1926.

PIRHING, E., *Ius Canonicum Nova Methodo Explicatum,* 5 vols., Dilingae, 1674–1678.

PRINCE, J., *The Diocesan Chancellor,* The Catholic University of America Canon Law Studies, n. 167, Washington, D. C.: The Catholic University of America Press, 1942.

REIFFENSTUEL, A., *Ius Canonicum Universum,* 6 vols., Romae, 1831–1834.

ROBERTI, F., *De Processibus,* 2 vols., Romae: Apud Aedes Facultatis Iuridicae ad S. Apollinaris, 1926.

ROSSI, I., *De Matrimonii Celebratione,* Romae: F. Pustet, 1924.

SANCHEZ, T., *De Sancto Matrimonio Disputationum Libri Decem, in Tres Tomos Distributi,* 3 vols., Antverpiae, 1626.

SCHAEFER, T., *De Religiosis,* Münster: Ex Officina Libraria Aschendorff, 1927.

SCHMALZGRUEBER, F., *Ius Ecclesiasticum Universum,* 5 vols. in 12, Romae, 1843–1845.

SCHROEDER, H. J., *Disciplinary Decrees of the General Councils,* St. Louis: B. Herder Book Co., 1937.

SIPOS, S., *Enchiridion Iuris Canonici,* 3. ed., Pecs: "Ex Typographia Haladas, R. T.," 1936.

VERMEERSCH, A., *Theologia Moralis,* 3. ed., 4 vols., Romae: Università Gregoriana, 1933.

VERMEERSCH, A.–CREUSEN, I., *Epitome Iuris Canonici,* 3 vols., Mechliniae—Romae: H. Dessain, 1934–1937. Vol. I, 6. ed., 1937; Vol. II, 5. ed., 1934; Vol. III, 5. ed., 1936.

VLAMING, TH. M., *Praelectiones Iuris Matrimonii,* 3. ed., 2 vols., Bussum in Hollandia: Sumptibus Societatis Editricis Anonymae Olim Paulus Brand, 1919–1921.

WALDRON, JOS. F., *The Minister of Baptism,* The Catholic University of America Canon Law Studies, n. 170, Washington, D. C.: The Catholic University of America Press, 1942.

WANENMACHER, F., *Canonical Evidence in Marriage Cases,* Philadelphia: Dolphin Press, 1935.

WERNZ, F., *Ius Decretalium,* 6 vols., Romae: Ex Typographia Polyglotta, 1906–1913.

WERNZ, F.–VIDAL, P., *Ius Canonicum,* 7 vols. in 8, Romae: apud Aedes Universitatis Gregorianae, 1927–1938. Vol. I, 1938; Vol. II, 2. ed., 1938; Vol. III, 1933; Vol. IV, Pars I, 1934; Vol. IV, Pars II, 1935; Vol. V, 2. ed., 1928; Vol. VI, 1927; Vol. VII, 1937.

WHALEN, DONALD W., *The Value of Testimonial Evidence in Matrimonial Procedure,* The Catholic University of America Canon Law Studies, n. 99, Washington, D. C.: The Catholic University of America Press, 1935.

WILLETT, ROBERT, *The Probative Value of Documents in Ecclesiastical Trials,* The Catholic University of America Canon Law Studies, n. 171, Washington, D. C.: The Catholic University of America Press, 1942.

WOYWOD, STANISLAUS, *A Practical Commentary on the Code of Canon Law,* 5. ed., 2 vols., New York: Jos. F. Wagner Inc., 1939.

PRINCIPAL ARTICLES

ANONYMOUS, "De la Confession Annuelle et de la Communion Pascale"—*Analecta Iuris Pontificii,* IV (1860), cols. 2260–2290.

ANONYMOUS, "Consilia et Responsa"—*Jus Pontificium,* XVI (1936), 111.

SCHAAF, V., "Proof of Baptism or of Dissolution of Marriage"—*AER,* XCIII (1935), 306–307.

SCHWEGLER, EDWARD, "A Practical Angle of Confirmation"—*AER,* XCVII (1937), 171–175.

PERIODICALS

Analecta Iuris Pontificii, Romae, 1852–1868; Parisiis, 1869–1891.

Archiv für katholische Kirchenrecht, Innsbruck, 1857–1861; Mainz, 1862–

American Ecclesiastical Review, The, Philadelphia, 1889–1943; Baltimore, 1944–

Irish Ecclesiastical Record, The, Dublin, 1864–

Jurist, The, Washington, D. C.: The Catholic University of America, 1941–

Jus Pontificium, Romae, 1921–

ABBREVIATIONS

AAS—Acta Apostolicae Sedis.

AER—The American Ecclesiastical Review.

ASS—Acta Sanctae Sedis.

Collectanea—Collectanea S. C. de Propaganda Fide.

Coll. Lac.—Collectio Lacensis.

Fontes—Codicis Iuris Canonici Fontes cura . . . Gasparri editi.

Jaffé—*Regesta Pontificum Romanorum* (edited by Ewald, Kaltenbrunner, Loewenfeld).

Mansi—*Sacrorum Conciliorum Nova et Amplissima Collectio.*

Pallottini—*Collectio Omnium Conclusionum et Resolutionum* etc.

Potthast—*Regesta Pontificum Romanorum.*

S. C. C.—Sacra Congregatio Concilii.

S. C. de Prop. Fide—Sacra Congregatio de Propaganda Fide.

S. C. de Sacramentis—Sacra Congregatio de Disciplina Sacramentorum.

S. C. pro Eccles. Orient.—Sacra Congregatio pro Ecclesia Orientali.

S. C. S. Off.—Suprema Congregatio Sancti Officii.

S. R. Rota—Sacra Romana Rota.

BIOGRAPHICAL NOTE

EUGENE H. SULLIVAN was born June 23, 1916, at Philadelphia, Pennsylvania. His studies for the priesthood were made at Saint Charles Seminary, Overbrook, Pennsylvania, the North American College, Rome, Italy, and the Catholic University of America, Washington, D. C. He was ordained to the Sacred Priesthood on December 20, 1940, at the Catholic University by the Most Reverend Joseph M. Corrigan, D.D. In 1939 he received the degree of Baccalaureate in Sacred Theology from the Pontifical Gregorian University in Rome, and in 1941, the degree of Licentiate in Sacred Theology from the Catholic University. He entered the Canon Law School of the latter institution in September, 1941. In May, 1942, he received the degree of Baccalaureate in Canon Law, and in May, 1943, the degree of Licentiate in Canon Law.

ALPHABETICAL INDEX

CANON LAW STUDIES*

1. Freriks, Rev. Celestine A., C.PP.S., J.C.D., Religious Congregations in Their External Relations, 121 pp., 1916.
2. Galliher, Rev. Daniel M., O.P., J.C.D., Canonical Elections, 117 pp., 1917.
3. Borkowski, Rev. Aurelius L., O.F.M., J.C.D., De Confraternitatibus Ecclesiasticis, 136 pp., 1918.
4. Castillo, Rev. Cayo, J.C.D., Disertacion Historico-Canonica sobre la Potestad del Cabildo en Sede Vacante o Impedida del Vicario Capitular, 99 pp., 1919 (1918).
5. Kubelbeck, Rev. William J., S.T.B., J.C.D., The Sacred Penitentiaria and Its Relation to Faculties of Ordinaries and Priests, 129 pp., 1918.
6. Petrovits, Rev. Joseph, J. C., S.T.D., J.C.D., The New Church Law on Matrimony, X-461 pp., 1919.
7. Hickey, Rev. John J., S.T.B., J.C.D., Irregularities and Simple Impediments in the New Code of Canon Law, 100 pp., 1920.
8. Klekotka, Rev. Peter J., S.T.B., J.C.D., Diocesan Consultors, 179 pp., 1920.
9. Wanenmacher, Rev. Francis, J.C.D., The Evidence in Ecclesiastical Procedure Affecting the Marriage Bond, 1920 (Printed 1935).
10. Golden, Rev. Henry Francis, J.C.D., Parochial Benefices in the New Code, IV-119 pp., 1921 (Printed 1925).
11. Koudelka, Rev. Charles J., J.C.D., Pastors, Their Rights and Duties According to the New Code of Canon Law, 211 pp., 1921.
12. Melo, Rev. Antonius, O.F.M., J.C.D., De Exemptione Regularium, X-188 pp., 1921.
13. Schaaf, Rev. Valentine Theodore, O.F.M., S.T.B., J.C.D., The Cloister, X-180 pp., 1921.
14. Burke, Rev. Thomas Joseph, S.T.D., J.C.D., Competence in Ecclesiastical Tribunals, IV-117 pp., 1922.
15. Leech, Rev. George Leo, J.C.D., A Comparative Study of the Constitution "Apostolicae Sedis" and the "Codex Juris Canonici," 179 pp., 1922.
16. Motry, Rev. Hubert Louis, S.T.D., J.C.D., Diocesan Faculties According to the Code of Canon Law, II-167 pp., 1922.
17. Murphy, Rev. George Lawrence, J.C.D., Delinquencies and Penalties in the Administration and the Reception of the Sacraments, IV-121 pp., 1923.

* Below n. 100 only the following numbers are still available: Nn. 3, 4, 9, 25, 34, 57 and 75. Beginning with n. 100 only the following are unavailable: Nn. 100-111 inclusive, and n. 113.

18. O'Reilly, Rev. John Anthony, S.T.B., J.C.D., Ecclesiastical Sepulture in the New Code of Canon Law, II-129 pp., 1923.
19. Michalicka, Rev. Wenceslas Cyril, O.S.B., J.C.D., Judicial Procedure in Dismissal of Clerical Exempt Religious, 107 pp., 1923.
20. Dargin, Rev. Edward Vincent, S.T.B., J.C.D., Reserved Cases According to the Code of Canon Law, IV-103 pp., 1924.
21. Godfrey, Rev. John A., S.T.B., J.C.D., The Right of Patronage According to the Code of Canon Law, 153 pp., 1924.
22. Hagedorn, Rev. Francis Edward, J.C.D., General Legislation on Indulgences, II-154 pp., 1924.
23. King, Rev. James Ignatius, J.C.D., The Administration of the Sacraments to Dying Non-Catholics, V-141 pp., 1924.
24. Winslow, Rev. Francis Joseph, O.F.M., J.C.D., Vicars and Prefects Apostolic, IV-149 pp., 1924.
25. Correa, Rev. Jose Servelion, S.T.L., J.C.D., La Potestad Legislativa de la Iglesia Catolica, IV-127 pp., 1925.
26. Dugan, Rev. Henry Francis, A.M., J.C.D., The Judiciary Department of the Diocesan Curia, 87 pp., 1925.
27. Keller, Rev. Charles Frederick, S.T.B., J.C.D., Mass Stipends, 167 pp., 1925.
28. Paschang, Rev. John Linus, J.C.D., The Sacramentals According to the Code of Canon Law, 129 pp., 1925.
29. Piontek, Rev. Cyrillus, O.F.M., S.T.B., J.C.D., De Indulto Exclaustrationis necnon Saecularizationis, XIII-289 pp., 1925.
30. Kearney, Rev. Richard Joseph, S.T.B., J.C.D., Sponsors at Baptism According to the Code of Canon Law, IV-127 pp., 1925.
31. Bartlett, Rev. Chester Joseph, A.M., LL.B., J.C.D., The Tenure of Parochial Property in the United States of America, V-108 pp., 1926.
32. Kilker, Rev. Adrian Jerome, J.C.D., Extreme Unction, V-425 pp., 1926.
33. McCormick, Rev. Robert Emmett, J.C.D., Confessors of Religious, VIII-266 pp., 1926.
34. Miller, Rev. Newton Thomas, J.C.D., Founded Masses According to the Code of Canon Law, VII-93 pp., 1926.
35. Roelker, Rev. Edward G., S.T.D., J.C.D., Principles of Privilege According to the Code of Canon Law, XI-166 pp., 1926.
36. Bakalarczyk, Rev. Richardus, M.I.C., J.U.D., De Novitiatu, VIII-208 pp., 1927.
37. Pizzuti, Rev. Lawrence, O.F.M., J.U.L., De Parochis Religiosis, 1927. (Not Printed.)
38. Bliley, Rev. Nicholas Martin, O.S.B., J.C.D., Altars According to the Code of Canon Law, XIX-132 pp., 1927.
39. Brown, Mr. Brendan Francis, A.B., LL.M., J.U.D., The Canonical Juristic Personality with Special Reference to its Status in the United States of America, V-212 pp., 1927.

40. CAVANAUGH, REV. WILLIAM THOMAS, C.P., J.U.D., The Reservation of the Blessed Sacrament, VIII-101 pp., 1927.
41. DOHENY, REV. WILLIAM J., C.S.C., A.B., J.U.D., Church Property: Modes of Acquisition, X-118 pp., 1927.
42. FELDHAUS, REV. ALOYSIUS H., C.PP.S., J.C.D., Oratories, IX-141 pp., 1927.
43. KELLY, REV. JAMES PATRICK, A.B., J.C.D., The Jurisdiction of the Simple Confessor, X-208 pp., 1927.
44. NEUBERGER, REV. NICHOLAS J., J.C.D., Canon 6 or the Relation of the Codex Juris Canonici to the Preceding Legislation, V-95 pp., 1927.
45. O'KEEFE, REV. GERALD MICHAEL, J.C.D., Matrimonial Dispensations, Powers of Bishops, Priests, and Confessors, VIII-232 pp., 1927.
46. QUIGLEY, REV. JOSEPH A. M., A.B., J.C.D., Condemned Societies, 139 pp., 1927.
47. ZAPLOTNIK, REV. JOHANNES LEO, J.C.D., De Vicariis Foraneis, X-142 pp., 1927.
48. DUSKIE, REV. JOHN ALOYSIUS, A.B., J.C.D., The Canonical Status of the Orientals in the United States, VIII-196 pp., 1928.
49. HYLAND, REV. FRANCIS EDWARD, J.C.D., Excommunication, Its Nature, Historical Development and Effects, VIII-181 pp., 1928.
50. REINMANN, REV. GERALD JOSEPH, O.M.C., J.C.D., The Third Order Secular of Saint Francis, 201 pp., 1928.
51. SCHENK, REV. FRANCIS J., J.C.D., The Matrimonial Impediments of Mixed Religion and Disparity of Cult, XVI-318 pp., 1929.
52. COADY, REV. JOHN JOSEPH, S.T.D., J.U.D., A.M., The Appointment of Pastors, VIII-150 pp., 1929.
53. KAY, REV. THOMAS HENRY, J.C.D., Competence in Matrimonial Procedure, VIII-164 pp., 1929.
54. TURNER, REV. SIDNEY JOSEPH, C.P., J.U.D., The Vow of Poverty, XLIX-217 pp., 1929.
55. KEARNEY, REV. RAYMOND A., A.B., S.T.D., J.C.D., The Principles of Delegation, VII-149 pp., 1929.
56. CONRAN, REV. EDWARD JAMES, A.B., J.C.D., The Interdict, V-163 pp., 1930.
57. O'NEILL, REV. WILLIAM H., J.C.D., Papal Rescripts of Favor, VII-218 pp., 1930.
58. BASTNAGEL, REV. CLEMENT VINCENT, J.U.D., The Appointment of Parochial Adjutants and Assistants, XV-257 pp., 1930.
59. FERRY, REV. WILLIAM A., A.B., J.C.D., Stole Fees, V-136 pp., 1930.
60. COSTELLO, REV. JOHN MICHAEL, A.B., J.C.D., Domicile and Quasi-Domicile, VII-201 pp., 1930.
61. KREMER, REV. MICHAEL NICHOLAS, A.B., S.T.B., J.C.D., Church Support in the United States, VI-136 pp., 1930.
62. ANGULO, REV. LUIS, C.M., J.C.D., Legislation de la Iglesia sobre la intencion en la application de la Santa Misa, VII-104 pp., 1931.

63. FREY, REV. WOLFGANG NORBERT, O.S.B., A.B., J.C.D., The Act of Religious Profession, VIII-174 pp., 1931.
64. ROBERTS, REV. JAMES BRENDAN, A.B., J.C.D., The Banns of Marriage, XIV-140 pp., 1931.
65. RYDER, REV. RAYMOND ALOYSIUS, A.B., J.C.D., Simony, IX-151 pp., 1931.
66. CAMPAGNA, REV. ANGELO, PH.D., J.U.D., Il Vicario Generale del Vescovo, VII-205 pp., 1931.
67. COX, REV. JOSEPH GODFREY, A.B., J.C.D., The Administration of Seminaries, VI-124 pp., 1931.
68. GREGORY, REV. DONALD J., J.U.D., The Pauline Privilege, XV-165 pp., 1931.
69. DONOHUE, REV. JOHN F., J.C.D., The Impediment of Crime, VII-110 pp., 1931.
70. DOOLEY, REV. EUGENE A., O.M.I., J.C.D., Church Law on Sacred Relics, IX-143 pp., 1931.
71. ORTH, REV. CLEMENT RAYMOND, O.M.C., J.C.D., The Approbation of Religious Institutes, 171 pp., 1931.
72. PERNICONE, REV. JOSEPH M., A.B., J.C.D., The Ecclesiastical Prohibition of Books, XII-267 pp., 1932.
73. CLINTON, REV. CONNELL, A.B., J.C.D., The Paschal Precept, IX-108 pp., 1932.
74. DONNELLY, REV. FRANCIS B., A.M., S.T.L., J.C.D., The Diocesan Synod, VIII-125 pp., 1932.
75. TORRENTE, REV. CAMILO, C.M.F., J.C.D., Las Procesiones Sagradas, V-145 pp., 1932.
76. MURPHY, REV. EDWIN J., C.PP.S., J.C.D., Suspension Ex Informata Conscientia, XI-122 pp., 1932.
77. MACKENZIE, REV. ERIC F., A.M., S.T.L., J.C.D., The Delict of Heresy in its Commission, Penalization, Absolution, VII-124 pp., 1932.
78. LYONS, REV. AVITUS E., S.T.B., J.C.D., The Collegiate Tribunal of First Instance, XI-147 pp., 1932.
79. CONNOLLY, REV. THOMAS A., J.C.D., Appeals, XI-195 pp., 1932.
80. SANGMEISTER, REV. JOSEPH V., A.B., J.C.D., Force and Fear as Precluding Matrimonial Consent, V-211 pp., 1932.
81. JAEGER, REV. LEO A., A.B., J.C.D., The Administration of Vacant and Quasi-Vacant Episcopal Sees in the United States, IX-229 pp., 1932.
82. RIMLINGER, REV. HERBERT T., J.C.D., Error Invalidating Matrimonial Consent, VII-79 pp., 1932.
83. BARRETT, REV. JOHN D. M., S.S., J.C.D., A Comparative Study of the Third Plenary Council of Baltimore and the Code, IX-221 pp., 1932.
84. CARBERRY, REV. JOHN J., PH.D., S.T.D., J.C.D., The Juridical Form of Marriage, X-177 pp., 1934.
85. DOLAN, REV. JOHN L., A.B., J.C.D., The Defensor Vinculi, XII-157 pp., 1934.

86. HANNAN, REV. JEROME D., A.M., S.T.D., LL.B., J.C.D., The Canon Law of Wills, IX-517 pp., 1934.
87. LEMIEUX, REV. DELISE A., A.M., J.C.D., The Sentence in Ecclesiastical Procedure, IX-131 pp., 1934.
88. O'ROURKE, REV. JAMES J., A.B., J.C.D., Parish Registers, VII-109 pp., 1934.
89. TIMLIN, REV. BARTHOLOMEW, O.F.M., A.M., J.C.D., Conditional Matrimonial Consent, X-381 pp., 1934.
90. WAHL, REV. FRANCIS X., A.B., J.C.D., The Matrimonial Impediments of Consanguinity and Affinity, VI-125 pp., 1934.
91. WHITE, REV. ROBERT J., A.B., LL.B., S.T.B., J.C.D., Canonical Ante-Nuptial Promises and the Civil Law, VI-152 pp., 1934.
92. HERRERA, REV. ANTONIO PARRA, O.C.D., J.C.D., Legislacion Ecclesiastica sobra el Ayuno y la Abstinencia, XI-191 pp., 1935.
93. KENNEDY, REV. EDWIN J., J.C.D., The Special Matrimonial Process in Cases of Evident Nullity, X-165 pp., 1935.
94. MANNING, REV. JOHN J., A.B., J.C.D., Presumption of Law in Matrimonial Procedure, XI-111 pp., 1935.
95. MOEDER, REV. JOHN M., J.C.D., The Proper Bishop for Ordination and Dimissorial Letters, VII-135 pp., 1935.
96. O'MARA, REV. WILLIAM A., A.B., J.C.D., Canonical Causes for Matrimonial Dispensations, IX-155 pp., 1935.
97. REILLY, REV. PETER, J.C.D., Residence of Pastors, IX-81 pp., 1935.
98. SMITH, REV. MARINER T., O.P., S.T.Lr., J.C.D., The Penal Law for Religious, VII-169 pp., 1935.
99. WHALEN, REV. DONALD W., A.M., J.C.D., The Value of Testimonial Evidence in Matrimonial Procedure, XIII-297 pp., 1935.
100. CLEARY, REV. JOSEPH F., J.C.D., Canonical Limitations on the Alienation of Church Property, VIII-141 pp., 1936.
101. GLYNN, REV. JOHN C., J.C.D., The Promoter of Justice, XX-337 pp., 1936.
102. BRENNAN, REV. JAMES H., S.S., M.A., S.T.B., J.C.D., The Simple Convalidation of Marriage, VI-135 pp., 1937.
103. BRUNINI, REV. JOSEPH BERNARD, J.C.D., The Clerical Obligations of Canons 139 and 142, X-121 pp., 1937.
104. CONNOR, REV. MAURICE, A.B., J.C.D., The Administrative Removal of Pastors, VIII-159 pp., 1937.
105. GUILFOYLE, REV. MERLIN JOSEPH, J.C.D., Custom, XI-144 pp., 1937.
106. HUGHES, REV. JAMES AUSTIN, A.B., A.M., J.C.D., Witnesses in Criminal Trials of Clerics, IX-140 pp., 1937.
107. JANSEN, REV. RAYMOND J., A.B., S.T.L., J.C.D., Canonical Provisions for Catechetical Instruction, VII-153 pp., 1937.
108. KEALY, REV. JOHN JAMES, A.B., J.C.D., The Introductory Libellus in Church Court Procedure, XI-121 pp., 1937.

109. McMANUS, REV. JAMES EDWARD, C.SS.R., J.C.D., The Administration of Temporal Goods in Religious Institutes, XVI-196 pp., 1937.
110. MORIARTY, REV. EUGENE JAMES, J.C.D., Oaths in Ecclesiastical Courts, X-115 pp., 1937.
111. RAINER, REV. ELIGIUS GEORGE, C.SS.R., J.C.D., Suspension of Clerics, XVII-249 pp., 1937.
112. REILLY, REV. THOMAS F., C.SS.R., J.C.D., Visitation of Religious, VI-195 pp., 1938.
113. MORIARITY, REV. FRANCIS E., C.SS.R., J.C.D., The Extraordinary Absolution from Censures, XV-334 pp., 1938.
114. CONNOLLY, REV. NICHOLAS P., J.C.D., The Canonical Erection of Parishes, X-132 pp., 1938.
115. DONOVAN, REV. JAMES JOSEPH, J.C.D., The Pastor's Obligation in Prenuptial Investigation, XII-322 pp., 1938.
116. HARRIGAN, REV. ROBERT J., M.A., S.T.B., J.C.D., The Radical Sanation of Invalid Marriages, VIII-208 pp., 1938.
117. BOFFA, REV. CONRAD HUMBERT, J.C.D., Canonical Provisions for Catholic Schools, VII-211 pp., 1939.
118. PARSONS, REV. ANSCAR JOHN, O.M.Cap., J.C.D., Canonical Elections, XII-236 pp., 1939.
119. REILLY, REV. EDWARD MICHAEL, A.B., J.C.D., The General Norms of Dispensation, XII-156 pp., 1939.
120. RYAN, REV. GERALD ALOYSIUS, A.B., J.C.D., Principles of Episcopal Jurisdiction, XII-172 pp., 1939.
121. BURTON, REV. FRANCIS JAMES, C.S.C., A.B., J.C.D., A Commentary on Canon 1125, X-222 pp., 1940.
122. MIASKIEWICZ, REV. FRANCIS SIGISMUND, J.C.D., Supplied Jurisdiction According to Canon 209, XII-340 pp., 1940.
123. RICE, REV. PATRICK WILLIAM, A.B., J.C.D., Proof of Death in Prenuptial Investigation, VIII-156 pp., 1940.
124. ANGLIN, REV. THOMAS FRANCIS, M.S., J.C.D., The Eucharistic Fast, VIII-183 pp., 1941.
125. COLEMAN, REV. JOHN JEROME, J.C.D., The Minister of Confirmation, VI-153 pp., 1941.
126. DOWNS, REV. JOSEPH EMMANUEL, A.B., J.C.D., The Concept of Clerical Immunity, XI-163 pp., 1941.
127. ESSWEIN, REV. ANTHONY ALBERT, J.C.D., Extrajudicial Penal Powers of Ecclesiastical Superiors, X-144 pp., 1941.
128. FARRELL, REV. BENJAMIN FRANCIS, M.A., S.T.L., J.C.D., The Rights and Duties of the Local Ordinary Regarding Congregations of Women Religious of Pontifical Approval, V-195 pp., 1941.
129. FEENEY, REV. THOMAS JOHN, A.B., S.T.L., J.C.D., Restitutio in Integrum, VI-169 pp., 1941.
130. FINDLAY, REV. STEPHEN WILLIAM, O.S.B., A.B., J.C.D., Canonical

Norms Governing the Deposition and Degradation of Clerics, XVII-279 pp., 1941.

131. Goodwine, Rev. John, A.B., S.T.L., J.C.D., The Right of the Church to Acquire Property, VIII-119 pp., 1941.

132. Heston, Rev. Edward Louis, C.S.C., Ph.D., S.T.D., J.C.D., The Alienation of Church Property in the United States, XII-222 pp., 1941.

133. Hogan, Rev. James John, A.B., S.T.L., J.C.D., Judicial Advocates and Procurators, XIII-200 pp., 1941.

134. Kealy, Rev. Thomas M., A.B., Litt.B., J.C.D., Dowry of Women Religious, IX-152 pp., 1941.

135. Keene, Rev. Michael James, O.S.B., J.C.D., Religious Ordinaries and Canon 198, V-164 pp., 1942.

136. Kerin, Rev. Charles A., S.S., M.A., S.T.B., J.C.D., The Privation of Christian Burial, XVI-279 pp., 1941.

137. Louis, Rev. William Francis, M.A., J.C.D., Diocesan Archives, X-101 pp., 1941.

138. McDevitt, Rev. Gilbert Joseph, A.B., J.C.D., Legitimacy and Legitimation, X-247 pp., 1941.

139. McDonough, Rev. Thomas Joseph, A.B., J.C.D., Apostolic Administrators, X-217 pp., 1941.

140. Meier, Rev. Carl Anthony, A.B., J.C.D., Penal Administration Procedure Against Negligent Pastors, XI-240 pp., 1941.

141. Schmidt, Rev. John Rogg, A.B., J.C.D., The Principles of Authentic Interpretation in Canon 17 of the Code of Canon Law, XII-331 pp., 1941.

142. Slafkosky, Rev. Andrew Leonard, A.B., J.C.D., The Canonical Episcopal Visitation of the Diocese, X-197 pp., 1941.

143. Swoboda, Rev. Innocent Robert, O.F.M., J.C.D., Ignorance in Relation to the Imputability of Delicts, IX-271 pp., 1941.

144. Dubé, Rev. Arthur Joseph, A.B., J.C.D., The General Principles for the Reckoning of Time in Canon Law, VIII-299 pp., 1941.

145. McBride, Rev. James T., A.B., J.C.D., Incardination and Excardination of Seculars, XX-585 pp., 1941.

146 Król, Rev. John T., J.C.D., The Defendant in Ecclesiastical Trials, XII-207 pp., 1942.

147. Comyns, Rev. Joseph J., C.SS.R., A.B., J.C.D., Papal and Episcopal Administration of Church Property, XIV-155 pp., 1942.

148. Barry, Rev. Garrett Francis, O.M.I., J.C.D., Violation of the Cloister, XII-260 pp., 1942.

149. Bolduc, Rev. Gatien, C.S.V., A.B., S.T.L., J.C.D., Les Études dans les Religions Cléricales, VIII-155 pp., 1942.

150. Boyle, Rev. David John, M.A., J.C.D., The Juridic Effects of Moral Certitude on Pre-Nuptial Guarantees, XII-188 pp., 1942.

151. Canavan, Rev. Walter Joseph, M.A., Litt.D., J.C.D., The Profession of Faith, XII-143 pp., 1942.

152. Desrochers, Rev. Bruno, A.B., Ph.L., S.T.B., J.C.D., Le Premier Concile Plénier de Québec et le Code de Droit Canonique, XIV–186 pp., 1942.
153. Dillon, Rev. Robert Edward, A.B., J.C.D., Common Law Marriage, X-148 pp., 1942.
154. Dodwell, Rev. Edward John, Ph.D., S.T.B., J.C.D., The Time and Place for the Celebration of Marriage, X-156 pp., 1942.
155. Donnellan, Rev. Thomas Andrew, A.B., J.C.D., The Obligation of the Missa pro Populo, VII-131 pp., 1942.
156. Eltz, Rev. Louis Anthony, A.B., J.C.L., Cooperation in Crime.
157. Gass, Rev. Sylvester Francis, M.A., J.C.D., Ecclesiastical Pensions, XI-206 pp., 1942.
158. Guiniven, Rev. John Joseph, C.SS.R., J.C.D., The Precept of Hearing Mass, XIV-188 pp., 1942.
159. Gulczynski, Rev. John Theophilus, J.C.D., The Desecration and Violation of Churches, X-126 pp., 1942.
160. Hammill, Rev. John Leo, M.A., J.C.D., The Obligations of the Traveler According to Canon 14, VIII-204 pp., 1942.
161. Haydt, Rev. John Joseph, A.B., J.C.D., Reserved Benefices, XI-148 pp., 1942.
162. Huser, Rev. Roger John, O.F.M., A.B., J.C.D., The Crime of Abortion in Canon Law, XII-187 pp., 1942.
163. Kearney, Rev. Francis Patrick, A.B., S.T.L., J.C.L., The Principles of Canon 1127.
164. Linahen, Rev. Leo James, S.T.L., J.C.D., De Absolutione Complicis In Peccato Turpi, 114 pp., 1942.
165. McCloskey, Rev. Joseph Aloysius, A.B., J.C.D., The Subject of Ecclesiastical Law According to Canon 12, XVII-246 pp., 1942.
166. O'Neill, Rev. Francis Joseph, C.SS.R., J.C.D., The Dismissal of Religious in Temporary Vows, XIII-220 pp., 1942.
167. Prince, Rev. John Edward, A.B., S.T.D., J.C.D., The Diocesan Chancellor, X-136 pp., 1942.
168. Riesner, Rev. Albert Joseph, C.SS.R., J.C.D., Apostates and Fugitives from Religious Institutes, IX-168 pp., 1942.
169. Stenger, Rev. Joseph Bernard, J.C.D., The Mortgaging of Church Property, 186 pp., 1942.
170. Waldron, Rev. Joseph Francis, A.B., J.C.D., The Minister of Baptism, XII-197 pp., 1942.
171. Willett, Rev. Robert Albert, J.C.D., The Probative Value of Documents in Ecclesiastical Trials, X-124 pp., 1942.
172. Woeber, Rev. Edward Martin, M.A., J.C.D., The Interpellations, XII-161 pp., 1942.
173. Benko, Rev. Matthew Aloysius, O.S.B., M.A., J.C.D., The Abbot *Nullius*.

174. Christ, Rev. Joseph James, M.A., S.T.L., J.C.D., Dispensation from Vindictive Penalties.
175. Clancy, Rev. Patrick M. J., O.P., A.B., S.T.Lr., J.C.D., The Local Religious Superior, X-229 pp., 1943.
176. Clarke, Rev. Thomas James, J.C.D., Parish Societies, XII-147 pp., 1943.
177. Connolly, Rev. John Patrick, S.T.L., J.C.D., Synodal Examiners and Parish Priest Consultors, X-223 pp., 1943.
178. Drumm, Rev. William Martin, A.B., J.C.D., Hospital Chaplains.
179. Flanagan, Rev. Bernard Joseph, A.B., S.T.L., J.C.D., The Canonical Erection of Religious Houses, X-147 pp., 1943.
180. Kelleher, Rev. Stephen Joseph, A.B., S.T.B., J.C.D., Discussions with non-Catholics: Canonical Legislation, X-93 pp., 1943.
181. Lewis, Rev. Gordian, C.P., J.C.D., Chapters in Religious Institutes, XII-169 pp., 1943.
182. Marx, Rev. Adolph, J.C.D., The Declaration of Nullity of Marriages Contracted Outside the Church, X-151 pp., 1943.
183. Matulenas, Rev. Raymond Anthony, O.S.B., A.B., J.C.L., Communication, a Source of Privileges.
184. O'Leary, Rev. Charles Gerard, C.SS.R., J.C.D., Religious Dismissed After Perpetual Profession, X-213 pp., 1943.
185. Power, Rev. Cornelius Michael, J.C.D., The Blessing of Cemeteries.
186. Shuhler, Rev. Ralph Vincent, O.S.A., J.C.D., Privileges of Regulars to Absolve and Dispense, XII-195 pp., 1943.
187. Ziolkowski, Rev. Thaddeus Stanislaus, A.B., J.C.D., The Consecration and Blessing of Churches, XII-151 pp., 1943.
188. Heneghan, Rev. John Joseph, S.T.D., J.C.D., The Marriages of Unworthy Catholics: Canons 1065 and 1066.
189. Carroll, Rev. Coleman Francis, M.A., S.T.L., J.C.L., Charitable Institutions.
190. Ciesluk, Rev. Joseph Edward, Ph.B., S.T.L., J.C.L., National Parishes in the United States.
191. Coburn, Rev. Vincent Paul, A.B., J.C.L., Marriages of Conscience.
192. Connors, Rev. Charles Paul, C.S.Sp., A.B., J.C.L., Extra-Judicial Procurators in the Code of Canon Law.
193. Coyle, Rev. Paul Raymond, A.B., J.C.L., Judicial Exceptions.
194. Fair, Rev. Bartholomew Francis, A.B., S.T.L., J.C.L., The Impediment of Abduction.
195. Gallagher, Rev. Thomas Raphael, O.P., A.B., S.T.Lr., J.C.L., The Examination of the Qualities of the Ordinand.
196. Gannon, Rev. John Mark, S.T.L., J.C.L., The Interstices Required for the Promotion to Orders.
197. Goldsmith, Rev. J. William, B.C.S., S.T.L., J.C.L., The Competence of Church and State over Marriage—Disputed Points,

198. Goodwine, Rev. Joseph Gerard, A.B., S.T.B., J.C.L., The Reception of Converts.
199. Kowalski, Rev. Romuald Eugene, O.F.M., A.B., J.C.L., Sustenance of Religious Houses of Regulars.
200. McCoy, Rev. Alan Edward, O.F.M., J.C.L., Force and Fear in Relation to Delictual Imputability and Penal Responsibility.
201. McDevitt, Rev. Vincent John, Ph.B., S.T.L., J.C.L., Perjury.
202. Martin, Rev. Thomas Owen, Ph.D., S.T.D., J.C.L., Adverse Possession, Prescription and Limitation of Actions: The Canonical "Praescriptio."
203. Miklosovic, Rev. Paul John, A.B., J.C.L., Attempted Marriages and Their Consequent Juridic Effects.
204. Mundy, Rev. Thomas Maurice, A.B., S.T.L., J.C.L., The Union of Parishes.
205. O'Dea, Rev. John Coyle, A.B., J.C.L., The Matrimonial Impediment of Nonage.
206. Olalia, Rev. Alexander Ayson, S.T.L., J.C.L., A Comparative Study of the Christian Constitution of States and the Constitution of the Philippine Commonwealth.
207. Poisson, Rev. Pierre-Marie, C.S.C., A.B., Ph.L., Th.L., J.C.L., Droits Patrimoniaux des Maisons et des Églises Religieuses.
208. Stadalnikas, Rev. Casimir Joseph, M.I.C., J.C.L., Reservation of Censures.
209. Sullivan, Rev. Eugene Henry, S.T.L., J.C.L., Proof of the Reception of the Sacraments.
210. Vaughan, Rev. William Edward, J.C.L., Constitutions for Diocesan Courts.
211. Lyons, Rev. Joseph Henry, J.C.L., The Joinder of Issue in Canonical Trials.

www.ingramcontent.com/pod-product-compliance
Lightning Source LLC
LaVergne TN
LVHW050228080826
844660LV00012B/496

* 9 7 8 0 8 1 3 2 2 3 9 3 3 *